THE MARIAN VOW

by Fr. Stefano Maria Manelli, FI

ACADEMY OF THE IMMACULATE
NEW BEDFORD, MA
2010

THE MARIAN VOW OF UNLIMITED CONSECRATION TO THE IMMACULATE: A SPIRITUAL PROFILE, is a book prepared for publication by the Franciscans of the Immaculate [marymediatrix.com], POB 3003, New Bedford, MA, 02741-3003.

© 2010 Franciscans of the Immaculate
All rights reserved

Nihil obstat quominus imprimatur
Most Rev. Mario Oliveri
Bishop of Albenga-Imperia
January 8, 2008, Albenga, Italy
Birthday of St. Maximilian M. Kolbe

Italian edition
Casa Mariana Editrice
2nd edition revised and enlarged:
January 1, 2008, Frigento (AV), Italy

Solemnity of Mary Most Holy, MOTHER OF GOD, 10th anniversary of the erection of the Franciscan Friars of the Immaculate as an Institute of Pontifical Right.

ISBN: 978-1-60114-049-4

THE MARIAN VOW OF UNLIMITED CONSECRATION TO THE IMMACULATE:

A SPIRITUAL PROFILE

Contents

Translator's note xi
Preface xiii
Introduction xv

Chapter 1
What is the Marian Vow? 1

Consecration without limits 1
Marian, saving action 5
Sublime sanctity and the salvation of souls 6

Chapter 2
Asceticism and Mysticism of the Marian Vow 9

She gives birth to "Jesus" in us 11
"Efficient" and "exemplary" cause 13
Radical "unlimitedness" 15
Love of the "pierced" Heart 18

Chapter 3
The Mission of the Marian Vow 21

To be transfigured into the Immaculate 21
Meditating so as to assimilate the Immaculate 23
Transfiguration into the Mediatrix 25
The missionary character of the Marian Vow 26

Chapter 4
The Marian Vow: "Presence" of the Immaculate 33

Marian "transubstantiation" and the Eucharistic life 34
A presence "analogous" to that of the Most Holy Trinity in the soul in the state of grace 37
Living this "presence" 39
"Proximity, possession, identification" 41
"Fixed idea," "drug," "obsession" 43
"But one heart in Her" 45
Take heart and do not be discouraged 46

Chapter 5
The Marian Vow and the Three Vows   49

The Marian-Seraphic "Vow"   49
The vow of obedience   51
The vow of poverty   54
The vow of chastity   55
The "proprium" of the Marian Vow   56
The "Matrix" of Trinitarian exemplarism   59

Chapter 6
The Marian Vow and the Fraternal Life   65

Marianize" the fraternal life   66
Beware of the 'itch for novelty' (cf. 2 Tm 4:3)   69
The "presence" of the Mother and Mediatrix   71
Uniting and identifying oneself with the Immaculate "Mother"   73

Chapter 7
The Marian Vow: The Life of Union with the Immaculate   81

St. Maximilian M. Kolbe   82
Saint Pio of Pietrelcina   83
Union between the Mother and Her children   84
Imitate Jesus in everything   86
Arriving at identification   87
Union: 24/7   89
Union with Our Lady… even unto the exchange of persons   90

Chapter 8
The Marian Vow and the "Immaculate Heart"   95

The Immaculate Heart: the mystery of Mary   96
Fatima and the Immaculate Heart   97
In the very Heart of the Immaculate   100
Fusion and christification   102
Jesus in the Eucharist—the "divine Heart" of Mary   103

Chapter 9
The Marian Vow and the Apostolic Life   107

The Marian dimension: its special value and importance   108

With every means available, on the offensive   109
Mass media: the choice of preference   112
Studying and speaking languages   113
"To lead the entire world to You"   114

Chapter 10
The Mystical Ascent of the Marian Vow   119

From Calvary to Tabor…   120
The "heart" of suffering   122
Trial upon trial…   124
Contemplative prayer   126
With Her, in Her, by Her…   129
In the Immaculate with the Holy Spirit   130

Chapter 11
The Marian Vow and the Priesthood   133

"Personifying" Jesus the Priest   133
"Grace upon grace"   134
Enamored of Jesus   136
A builder of the Church   137
The father of souls   138
In the hour of trial   139
A totally Marian priest   141

Chapter 12
The Marian Vow and the Devotional Life of the Franciscans of the Immaculate   145

Liturgical prayer   145
Contemplative prayer   146
The celebration of the Eucharist   147
Communion with the Immaculate   148
Visits to the Blessed Sacrament   149
Sacramental Confession   150
Continual Marian prayer   151
The Holy Rosary   152

Conclusion   155
Works Cited   161

TRANSLATOR'S NOTE

It is with joy and trepidation that we present this English translation of Fr. Stefano Maria Manelli's *Il Voto Mariano*. It is a joy because this book is utterly unique and inspired. As the Founder and Father General of the entire family of the Franciscans of the Immaculate (Friars, Sisters, Poor Clares, Tertiaries, and M.I.M.), Fr. Stefano has distilled and put into writing for his children the illumination he has received over the decades about the *Marian Vow*. This work is the fruit of his life of prayer, study, and missionary activity. It is the fruit of his profound union with the Immaculate Heart of Mary.

On the other hand, there is a bit of trepidation in presenting an English rendering of such a sublime text for two reasons. First, many of the friars and sisters already know Italian and will readily see that something has been lost in the translation—this is the downfall of any translation. Translating is a work of comprehension and expression, which at times requires creativity and compromise in order to express the original material in a readable fashion in another language (e.g., in the Italian many of the paragraphs are one long sentence; whereas in English we tend to divide into shorter sentences while maintaining the same concept throughout the paragraph). While some crumbs will always fall off the table even in the best of translations, we have tried to keep the substantial content on the table and are hopeful that Fr. Stefano's message will resound loud and clear in English.

Secondly, Fr. Stefano has a charism which comes from above, namely from the Holy Spirit through the Immaculate Heart of Mary. This means that many of the ideas and terms used in the Italian are without precedent and cannot be found in any Italian dictionary, let alone an Italian-English dictionary. Therefore, new words had to be sculpted in English in order to translate his inspirations. At times there was simply no easy solution and so much was lost in the translation that we felt the need to insert a footnote giving the original Italian term both as an apology for our incapacity to translate the term well and as an aid to those who might benefit from a clearer glimpse at the concept or word in the original Italian. All the footnotes have been added by the translator. Also, at times we felt the need to add a brief explanation of a concept or term in brackets [everything in brackets is a clarification or explanation]. Works cited in short form or with abbreviations can be found fully listed in the bibliography at the end of the volume.

All Old Testament quotes are taken from the Douay-Rheims Bible [*Haydock Catholic Family Bible and Commentary*, Edward Dunigan and Brother, NY (1859), photographically reproduced by Catholic Treasures CA (2006)] and all New Testament quotes from the Confraternity Revision of the New Testament [*The New Testament of Our Lord and Savior Jesus Christ*, reprinted by Scepter Publisher, NY (2005)].

With the exception of Scripture quotes, all other quotes have been translated directly from the Italian citations even where English translations are available elsewhere. Hence we have retained Fr. Stefano's references to the Italian editions of the works cited. Many of these works are available in English (e.g., *True Devotion to Mary, The Franciscan Omnibus of Sources, etc.*).

A few points should be made about the format of this work. The italics and the frequent quotation marks are Fr. Stefano's—not the translator's nor the editor's. He uses italics in the Italian original to highlight certain quotes and ideas; we have chosen not to tamper with the Founder's style of emphasis. Please note that for added emphasis in an italicized quote he will sometimes 'un-italicize' words, a sort of emphasis within an emphasis. Regarding quotation marks around certain terms, Fr. Stefano uses these to indicate a certain novelty or qualification in the term being used (e.g., "transubstantiate," "christify," etc.).

Furthermore, in the Italian original certain parts are set off with indentation and a different font. This, too, is a style of Fr. Stefano. It is his way of indicating corollary material to the topic at hand. Consequently, this means that larger quotes are not indented as is the editorial standard in English nowadays.

Special thanks to all of those who have proofread the text and offered their timely suggestions and corrections. In the end, all the mistakes and imperfections of the English translation are solely the translator's; whereas all of the "milk and honey" that flows forth from these pages are from the heart of our Common Father whose heart beats in unison with that of the Immaculate. May these pages redound to the glory of God and the Immaculate! May they find an echo in the lives and hearts of the reader! So be it.

PREFACE

There are many questions that have come to the fore about the *Marian Vow* of unlimited consecration to the Immaculate (also called the "proper" or distinctive vow) which characterizes the religious Institute of the Franciscan Friars of the Immaculate, the Franciscan Sisters of the Immaculate and the Poor Clares of the Immaculate, as well as the individual members, both lay and consecrated, of the Mission of the Immaculate Mediatrix (the M.I.M.).

There are questions about the history of this *Marian Vow* which, formulated as such, has no precedent in any other religious Order or Institute. There are questions about its content and dogmatic character. There are questions about its juridical and moral significance. There are questions about its orthopraxy, that is to say, how to put it into practice and so on.

In this work, *reworked and further developed*, the *Marian Vow* is presented primarily within the concise framework of a "spiritual profile." Examined and deepened in its fundamental, constitutive aspects, the *Marian Vow* is seen in the light of Marian theology, spiritual theology and Franciscan theology.

These fundamental and essential aspects form the basic "profile" of the spirituality of the *Marian Vow*. One could also speak of this work in terms of a rough sketch of that grand design of the spirituality of the *Marian Vow*. This sketch, in turn, must then be developed line by line in the even larger picture or project of the Franciscan life sealed and animated by the *Marian Vow*.

This ever developing "profile" will serve to indicate the spiritual features of those consecrated with the *Marian Vow*. It will present the characteristic physiognomy and make-up that constitute the relation of the *Marian Vow* to the interior and exterior dimensions of their life. It will present the *Marian Vow* in both its essence and activity (*esse et operari*), that is, in its entitative-constitutive as well as its dynamic-apostolic dimensions.

Of particular importance is the "profile" of the profound contact and unifying bond between the *Marian Vow* and the reality of the religious life of the Franciscans and Poor Clares taken in its primary and essential elements: the religious profession with its three vows, the community life, the apostolic activity and the priesthood. All of these receive from the *Marian Vow* a light and a soul which marianizes the Seraphic form of life of the Franciscans of the Immaculate, friars and sisters; a form of life which must bring all of its members to the most pure christification.

The rough sketch which results, taken as a whole, gives a clear idea of the much bigger picture of the spirituality of the *Marian Vow* of unlimited consecration to the Immaculate. This vow has a wealth of value. One could say, in fact, that it enriches the spiritual life in such an extraordinary manner as to bring it to the absolute peak of all spirituality, placing it upon the summit of the entire ascetical and mystical journey. After all, we are speaking of a journey which brings about the transfiguration of the person into the Immaculate, that is, into She who is the *"most holy Woman," the one who is "full of grace"* (Lk 1:28), the one who has "the face which most resembles that of Christ."[1]

The splendid models of this *marianiziation-christification* in accordance with the potential and vitality of the *Marian Vow* are, above all, the four Patron Saints of the *Franciscans of the Immaculate:* the Seraphic Father St. Francis of Assisi, the Seraphic Mother St. Clare of Assisi, St. Maximilian Mary Kolbe and St. Pio of Pietrelcina. These four models are a paradigm of superlative sanctity and beauty.

To reach that perfect and sublime "conformity" to Christ realized through the Immaculate, to cooperate in the universal mediation of grace of the Immaculate, Coredemptrix with Her Redeemer Son, to cooperate in the salvation of the whole of humanity: this constitutes the highest point of the actualization of the mystery of the Incarnation and Redemption in any single creature, in a religious Order, and even in the whole Church. This peak emerges through transformation in the mysteries of the Immaculate Conception and universal mediation of Mary; it is brought to completion by the salvation of all unto the supreme glory of the Most Holy Trinity.

Reflection, meditation, study, and prayer, under the guidance of the Holy Spirit, will help us to penetrate evermore deeply the *Marian Vow* which is centered in the ineffable mystery of the Immaculate Conception, in She who is the Paradise of God the Father, the Son, and the Holy Spirit.

---

1 Dante, *Divine Comedy: Paradiso*, [hereafter cited *Paradiso*], XXXII, 85–86.

INTRODUCTION

The *Marian Vow* of unlimited consecration to the Immaculate is a gift *"from above"* (Jas 1:17). It is a gift which is the fruit of an initial divine inspiration of the greatest Marian Apostle and Franciscan Martyr of the twentieth century: St. Maximilian M. Kolbe.

The initial inspiration which the Saint received, in fact, is that of a *fourth vow* by which the friar, in consecrating himself, dedicates himself without reserve to the *"missionary character"*[2] [of the Church in general and the Franciscan Order in particular]. Thus, he becomes an *instrument* in the hands of the Immaculate according to the obedience he receives from his superiors who can send him to any "mission" whatsoever.

It is from this root, that is to say, from the *fourth vow* of a Marian-missionary character, that the *Marian Vow* has blossomed forth for the Franciscans of the Immaculate, friars and sisters. It is a "proper" religious vow of unlimited consecration to the Immaculate. This vow has sprung forth from the very soul of the Seraphic Father St. Francis. The Immaculate Herself made him worthy to conceive and give birth anew to evangelical life in the Seraphic Order when he dwelt at the *Portiuncula* of St. Mary of the Angels.

The Seraphic Doctor, St. Bonaventure, describes this ineffable grace very well: "In the Church of the Virgin Mother of God, therefore, dwelt Her servant Francis and he petitioned insistently with continual cries Her [sic] who had conceived the *Word, full of grace*, that She might deign to be his advocate. And the Mother of mercy, obtained by Her merits that he himself would conceive and bring forth the spirit of evangelical truth."[3]

From St. Francis this precious gift, which emerges in the *Marian Vow*, was given St. Maximilian and then to our religious family of the *Franciscans of the Immaculate*. It has been given in order to transfigure those consecrated to the Immaculate by "transubstantiating" them into the very person of the Immaculate. In this way, the most perfect Franciscan life is realized in accord with St. Francis and the *Seraphic*

---

[2] *missionarietà* in Italian and translated as "missionary character, dimension, or quality" throughout this text.
[3] Bonaventure, *Legenda maior*, Part I, Ch. 3, 1 (*Fonti Francescane* [here forward, FF], 1051).

Rule, a life which arrives at the most sublime christification, which is that of the Immaculate Herself.

The *Marian Vow*, therefore, is no longer distinguished by the "missionary character" alone, but also by the totality of the religious life itself according to the *Seraphic Rule*. Through the *Marian Vow* this life and *Rule* become utterly "Mary-formed"[4] for the highest and most perfect "conformity-to-Christ,"[5] namely, that of the Immaculate Herself. Thus, this way of life is fruitful for the salvation of all souls unto the supreme glory of the Most Holy Trinity. *"When we shall have become Her,"* writes St. Maximilian, *"our entire religious life too and its sources shall be of Her and Her alone."*[6]

Hence, it can also be said that the *Marian Vow* bears with it the very same "Christ-conformity" of the Immaculate which, for the Franciscan of the Immaculate, becomes the ideal to strive after through unlimited consecration to Her. As such, the *Marian Vow* renders each Franciscan of the Immaculate Her *"absolute property,"* as St. Maximilian expressly states,[7] even to the point of being lost in Her, being transfigured and "transubstantiated" entirely into Her, as again St. Maximilian teaches.[8]

Consequently, the *Marian Vow* is the first of the four religious vows which are pronounced in the religious Profession of the Franciscans of the Immaculate according to the *Seraphic Rule*. It constitutes the Marian source of the whole seraphic life of christification. It can be said that the *Marian Vow* prolongs the mystery of the redemptive Incarnation of the Word which occurred in the Heart and womb of the Immaculate.

The *Marian Vow*, then, is readily understood to be a special grace flowing forth from the very Heart of the Mother and Mediatrix of all graces. We are speaking of a vow whose goal is to articulate the maximum of seraphic love. That maximum is the dedication of man's entire heart, that is, the fullness of the whole person's vital love. It could also rightly be called the vow of unlimited love for the Immaculate, a love directed through Her to God and to all creatures, a love which is ultimately directed towards the salvation of all souls in Christ and in the Church for the greatest glory of the Most Holy Trinity.

---

[4] *mariaforme* in Italian.
[5] *cristiformità* in Italian, translated as "conformity-to-Christ" or "Christ-conformity" throughout this text.
[6] St. Maximilian's writing: *Scritti* [hereafter cited SK] 486
[7] SK 1160
[8] Cf. SK 508

The *Marian Vow* of unlimited consecration to the Immaculate, therefore, is a vow "proper" to the Franciscans of the Immaculate, friars and sisters. It is rooted in the *Seraphic Rule* and deepened and developed in all its charismatic content of grace (which is also extended and shared as a private vow among the secular members of the Mission of the Immaculate Mediatrix, called the M.I.M.).

The *Marian Vow* is, as a matter of fact, the primary *raison d'être*:

- of the Franciscan Friars of the Immaculate who are a new branch of the First Order of St. Francis in historical continuity, therefore, with the *O.F.M.s*, the *Conventuals* and the *Capuchins*, by virtue of the exact same form of religious life according to the *Seraphic Rule* confirmed by Pope Honorius III;

- of the Franciscan Sisters of the Immaculate who constitute an historical novelty of great importance and worth because they are the first religious Institute of women to profess the Rule of St. Francis, that is, the very *Regula Bullata* of the First Order. It can and must be said, therefore, that the Franciscan Sisters of the Immaculate, united to the Order of Minors by the same *Regula Bullata*, represent the very first *First Order of women*. Who does not grasp the great value and singular merit of such a first-fruit?

On a par with the other three religious vows of obedience, poverty, and chastity, this *Marian Vow* is specifically an essential constitutive vow of the spirituality and discipline of the Franciscans of the Immaculate, friars and sisters. And it can also be said symbolically that the *Marian Vow* is comparable to the Marian *Portiuncula* of St. Mary of the Angels, that entirely Marian womb of Franciscanism so cherished by St. Maximilian and brought to fruition, according to the divine will, by this new little religious family of the Franciscans of the Immaculate, friars and sisters (together with the secular members who make up the Association M.I.M., and other individuals).

In reflecting on the entire program of life linked with the *Marian Vow*, it can rightly be said that as the *Portiuncula* of St. Mary of the Angels in Assisi is considered the completely Marian "womb" of Franciscanism, so, too, the *Marian Vow*, assimilated with the *Portiuncula*, can be considered the completely Marian womb of the Franciscans of the Immaculate. The latter, then, have developed the Marian dimension of Franciscan spirituality and life by drawing forth afresh from the fountainhead of the *Seraphic Rule* and the life of the Seraphic Father.

The *Marian Vow* is, therefore, what distinguishes the Franciscan of the Immaculate, friar or sister, and is *"the soul of the Constitutions,"* as St. Maximilian said.[9] This distinctive feature appears even visibly by the Miraculous Medal which the Franciscan of the Immaculate wears over his heart, attached to a gray-blue habit, and by the additional "knot" on the cord. A Franciscan of the Immaculate can be recognized immediately and easily: he always wears the habit, carries the Medal of the Immaculate visibly over his heart, and has the additional knot on the cord.

Consequently, it can also be said that in relation to the other three vows, the *Marian Vow* has a distinctive, specific character immediately manifesting the *proprium* of the charism, the "novelty" and the specific spirituality of the Franciscans of the Immaculate. The Institute is rooted *in toto* in the Franciscan charism and spirituality common to all Franciscans of the First Order.

During the time when St. Maximilian was permitted to speak and write on this theme he presented the *Marian Vow*—which he called the "fourth vow"—as limitless consecration of oneself to the Immaculate whose unlimited character prompted one to accept the call to go to the mission lands, even the most difficult and dangerous, even where *martyrdom* is expected.[10]

Unfortunately, St. Maximilian was not able to leave us an organic and articulated treatise on the *Marian Vow*, but only various insights scattered throughout a small part of his writings (ten of his *Letters*). These, nonetheless, are sufficient to gather the substance of the *Marian Vow* in its constitutive elements. His insights are elaborated and united in a single synthesis in the Constitutions of the Franciscans of the Immaculate, friars and sisters. As such, their potentiality in content and worth are developed and enriched for a Franciscan life in accord with the *Seraphic Rule,* a life fully "marianized" and "christified" in the school and in the footsteps of St. Francis, St. Clare, St. Maximilian, and St. Pio of Pietrelcina.

---

[9] SK 485
[10] Cf. SK 395, 398, 399, 402, 409, 412, 419, 492, 588, 653

CHAPTER 1
WHAT IS THE MARIAN VOW?

According to its exact canonical formulation, the *Marian Vow*, in its essence, is the solemn promise made to God through religious profession according to the *Regula Bullata* of St. Francis of Assisi of unlimited consecration of oneself to the Immaculate as Her *"absolute property"*[11] in order to hasten the coming of Christ's Kingdom in the whole world.

There are two constitutive elements of the *Marian Vow*:

> a) the unlimited donation-consecration of oneself to the Immaculate as Her "absolute property" according to the form of life of the *Seraphic Rule* approved by Pope Honorius III;

> b) apostolic Marian action for the coming of the Kingdom of Christ in the whole world.

These two elements are related to one another as *being* and *acting*,[12] as having and giving away. They carry within themselves the dynamism of divine grace as entity and energy directed towards one's personal sanctification and the salvation of all for the maximum glory of God.

Let us briefly analyze these two primary, constitutive elements.

CONSECRATION WITHOUT LIMITS

Unlimited consecration of oneself to the Immaculate as Her *"absolute property"* means the realization of the full union of love with the Immaculate to the point of maximum assimilation and identification with Her.

---

[11] SK 1160
[12] In Latin *essere et operare*.

The *"absolute property"* of the Immaculate *par excellence* is the Infant Jesus, enclosed within the womb of the Immaculate, Ever-Virgin. After Him is St. Joseph, Husband of Mary, who could be called the unrivaled *icon* of the *Marian Vow* by his ineffable spousal and virginal union with the Immaculate rendering him indissolubly *one* with Her.

This union with Mary through the *Marian Vow* moves the soul towards that perfection which is the identification of the consecrated person with the Immaculate, his "annihilation," in a certain sense, in the Immaculate and his mystical "transubstantiation" into Her so that "She alone" may live in him. This is the express teaching of St. Maximilian M. Kolbe:

> *"She penetrates our soul and directs its faculties with unlimited power. We truly belong to Her. Therefore, we are with Her always and everywhere... But what must we think of ourselves? Let us disappear in Her! May She alone remain, and we in Her, a part of Her. But is it licit for us, miserable creatures that we are, to rave in this manner? Nonetheless, this is the truth, the reality."*[13]

And further still:

> *"We are Hers, of the Immaculate, unlimitedly Hers, perfectly Hers; we are, as it were,* Her very self [...] *We want to belong to the Immaculate to the point that not only nothing may remain in us that is not of Her, but that we may become annihilated, as it were, in Her,* changed *in Her, transubstantiated in Her, that She Herself may remain."*[14]

Here we enter fully the realm of mysticism. And this is the primary path of the Franciscan of the Immaculate who rises through the practice of perfect imitation of the virtues of the Immaculate to arrive at the mystical identification with the Immaculate. Thus, he passes through all of the ascetical and mystical phases of the active and passive purifications which bring him to the mystical death of self in the transforming and consummating union.

At this terminal point of the spiritual ascent we can truly say that those who have taken the *Marian Vow* are mystically "annihilated" in the Immaculate and "transubstantiated" into the Immaculate. This is

---

[13] SK 461
[14] SK 508

so true that we can say, paraphrasing what St. Paul on the union of the Christian with Christ: they no longer live, but the Immaculate lives and remains in them: *"She alone."*

"She alone," writes St. Maximilian, *"must instruct each of us in every instant; She must direct us, transform us into Herself, in such wise that it is no longer we who live, but She in us, just as Jesus lives in Her and the Father in the Son. Let us grant Her permission to do in us and by means of us whatever She desires, and She will surely accomplish miracles of grace: we will become saints and great saints..."*[15]

Here, in effect, is realized the grace of the living and sanctifying *presence* of the Immaculate: not a physical *presence*, but a spiritual one; not just an ideal *presence*, but a real one; a *presence* which pervades the entire soul of the person consecrated. It could be said that, in a certain sense, it is a *presence* analogous to the presence of the Most Holy Trinity in the soul living in grace.

If the *Marian Vow* is, in fact, a *vow*, this means that it is a *knot*, that is to say, a vow which establishes a binding union between those consecrated and the Immaculate in order to transform them into Her to the point of transfiguring and transubstantiating them into Her. This gradually brings them to become entirely Her so that, in a mystical manner, nothing finally remains in them except: *"She alone."*

Provided there is faithful correspondence on their part, the *Marian Vow* carries within itself the grace of this living *presence* of the Immaculate. This *presence* thoroughly pervades the mind, the heart, and the will of the consecrated soul. St. Maximilian was a perfect model of this; he kept the Immaculate really present and active as that *"fixed thought"* in his mind, as that *"mad love"* in his heart, and as that *"feverish action"* in his will.[16]

It can and must be said that those who reach this level of transformation and identification in the Immaculate by faithfully living the *Marian Vow* make the Immaculate fully and truly present. Thus, mystically speaking, they no longer live, but the Immaculate lives in each of them. This is precisely the very essence of *transubstantiation* into the Immaculate.

This means, however, that they, in being perfectly identified with the Immaculate, will realize in themselves a *christification* so complete and a *conformity-to-Christ* so perfect as to be able to have, like Mary, "the face that most resembles Christ," as Dante Alighieri

---

[15] SK 556, 643
[16] Respectively *idea fissa*, *amore folle*, and *azione febbrile* in Italian.

says in speaking of the divine Mother.[17] In other words, they will have reached the highest and most sublime union and conformity of love to Jesus, which is that of the Immaculate Herself. *"As Jesus lives in Her,"* writes St. Maximilian, so Jesus will live in anyone who is faithful to the *Marian Vow*. This *christification—conformity-to-Christ—*is the greatest and most sublime possible, as St. Maximilian explains when speaking of the love of the Immaculate for God:

> *"The Immaculate is so united to God through love that She is elevated not only above all of the Saints, but even above the Angels, the Archangels, the Cherubim, the Seraphim; hence an unlimited love towards the Immaculate lifts us up to Her (and unites us to Her through love), above... all of these... What is unlimited love for the Immaculate? She is the One closest to God, while we are closest to Her and, consequently, through Her to God Himself. God has given us this white ladder and He desires that we may come to Him by climbing it, or rather that She, after having embraced us tightly to Her motherly bosom, may carry us to God."*[18]

To what heights the Immaculate desires to carry Her "property!" Thus, St. Maximilian had every reason to rejoice when he asserted: *"may the knowledge of belonging completely to the Immaculate fill us with boundless joy."*[19]

Anyone who faithfully lives the *Marian Vow*, therefore, can repeat St. Paul's words to the Galatians, extended to include and be completed in Mary: *"'It is no longer I that live, but Christ lives in me' (2:20) through the Immaculate and in the Immaculate."* This means to live Christ in the most perfect and sublime form because, as St. Maximilian brilliantly teaches, *"In the womb of the Immaculate the soul is reborn in the form of Jesus Christ,"*[20] by the working of the Holy Spirit. Once born, the soul's entire upbringing and growth is entrusted to Her as well. Thus, St. Maximilian goes on to say, *"She must nourish the soul with the milk of Her grace, lovingly care for it, and educate it just as She nourished, cared for, and educated Jesus. On Her knees the soul must learn how to know and love Jesus. It must draw love*

---

[17] *Paradiso*, XXXII, 85–86.
[18] SK 461
[19] SK 834
[20] SK 1295

for *Him from Her Heart, or even love Him with Her Heart and become like unto Him by means of love.*"[21]

In this way, provided that those who have taken the *Marian Vow* are generous and faithful in corresponding to being the absolute property of the Immaculate without reserve, it can also be said that they become all the more the property of Jesus, just as the Immaculate is the property of Jesus; and they therefore become the property of God[22] who is the ultimate goal of the entire journey of grace.

MARIAN, SAVING ACTION

The fruit of the ascetical and mystical journey of unlimited consecration to the Immaculate, therefore, is our transformation in Christ, like Mary, in such a perfect manner that each of us can be considered, as it were, *"She Herself living, speaking and acting,"* as St. Maximilian teaches.[23]

From this expression of St. Maximilian we can immediately grasp the saving action flowing from our "being." This action flows from that apostolic and missionary dynamic of being the "absolute property" of the Immaculate, of being transfigured in Her. In other words, the *Marian Vow* makes Mary "present" and "active"; it is Mary who lives and acts through each of us; or more precisely, it is Mary *"living, speaking and acting."*

Thus, the apostolic activity of those consecrated to the Immaculate by the *Marian Vow* bursts forth from this source. St. Bernard teaches, and St. Louis M. de Montfort and St. Maximilian confirm, that God, with Christ, has entrusted to Mary His saving will for all humanity. This being the case, those consecrated to the Immaculate and who have become "other Marys" are called to participate, cooperate, and make this universal saving will their own. They are called to save their brothers and sisters, be ready to give themselves entirely, and even be ready *"to go into the whole world"* (Mk 16:15), impelled by a generosity without limits.

The universal, salvific Coredemption accomplished by the Immaculate, starting with the *Fiat* of the Annunciation and culminating with the *Stabat Mater* at the foot of the Cross on Calvary, becomes constant "maternal mediation" of all graces which are to be

---
[21] Ibid.
[22] Cf. SK 1226
[23] SK 486

dispensed to all mankind. Mary's application of the saving merits of Redemption to mankind shall endure throughout man's journey, even until the end of time. It shall always continue in a synergy of love and action with the Church who looks to the Immaculate and aspires to Her in order to become ever "more similar to her exalted Model"(LG 65).

So it is that with the *Marian Vow* all of the Franciscans of the Immaculate "lose" themselves in the Immaculate and arrive at identifying themselves entirely with Her. Each of them becomes a partaker of Her "mission." What is more, they share in the very universal saving "mission" of the Immaculate Mediatrix as Her *"docile instruments,"* always ready and untiring in sacrificing themselves in bringing the Savior to every human heart that beats on the face of the earth:[24] always with the Immaculate, in the Immaculate, and *"through the Immaculate."*[25]

St. Maximilian literally says, *"The Immaculate must be introduced into the hearts of men, so that She may erect within them the throne of Her Son, so that She may rouse them to a knowledge of Him and inflame them with love for the Most Sacred Heart of Jesus."*[26]

SUBLIME SANCTITY AND THE SALVATION OF SOULS

One of the first conclusions drawn from this brief analysis of the two constitutive elements of the *Marian Vow—being and action—*is this: living the *Marian Vow* with generous and faithful dedication means bringing about that holiness which is most sublime and the salvation of souls which is most extensive, all for the greatest glory of God. Sanctity so sublime and salvation so far-reaching: these two elements are intrinsically linked. They are so interdependent that one cannot exist without the other, and both of them are directed towards the greatest glory of God.

To summarize, then, the *Marian Vow* entails:

    a) unlimited consecration to the Immaculate as Her "absolute property," lived according to the form of the *Seraphic Rule*;

    b) the call to and direct participation in the very universal, saving mission of the Immaculate Mediatrix;

---

[24] Cf. SK 603
[25] SK 1231
[26] SK486

c) that missionary character extending to every field for the salvation of the brethren in every corner of the world which seeks to carry the Immaculate, who is the Mother of Jesus the Savior, into their hearts.

But the analysis must continue if we are to gather in the rich harvest that this *Marian Vow* carries within itself. The *Marian Vow* makes the religious life and apostolate of the Franciscans of the Immaculate all the more precious. It enriches and expands the Christian life, too, for those who by means of it, desire to consecrate themselves without limit in order to become the "absolute property" of the Immaculate.

The spiritual theology of the Franciscan pathway, in particular, and the mystical-ascetical journey, in general, offers contributions of great worth and presents important aspects of the content of the *Marian Vow*. This is so because the *Marian Vow* engages all of the powers of the consecrated soul, marianizing them so as to christify them in the manner which is most ineffably holy.

At this point in our study, we want to enter upon this pathway and rapidly make this journey. In this way, we will be able to delineate and analyze many of the more significant and enlightening points about the *Marian Vow* which is a gem with millions of beautiful facets.

CHAPTER 2
ASCETICISM AND MYSTICISM OF THE MARIAN VOW

The *Marian Vow* of unlimited consecration to the Immaculate entails a vigorous, radical, and complete asceticism. In terms which can be immediately grasped, this means two things which are essential and practical:

1. Eliminate every defect, even minimal, which is unbecoming to the surpassing holiness and immaculate purity of the Mother of God. If we indeed are called to be the Immaculate's "property," it is obvious that we need to be a pure and noble "property" which is assimilated to Her as a "little church," so to speak, *"not having spot or wrinkle"* (Eph 5:27). St. Maximilian writes, *"I prayed to the Immaculate that She might purify my thoughts, my words, and my actions from all that does not come from Her."*[27] His companion during formation, Fr. Joseph Pal, attests that "Maximilian fled from even the smallest sin: in six years of living at college with him I never saw him commit even the smallest voluntary sin."[28]

2. Clothe oneself, both interiorly and exteriorly, with the very virtues and gifts most prized in the Immaculate: namely, the theological and cardinal virtues, the moral and religious virtues, and the gifts of the Holy Spirit. In this way, we are transfigured entirely in Her, thus becoming, as it were, *"She Herself living, speaking, and acting in this world,"* as St. Maximilian M. Kolbe expressly states.[29]

---

[27] SK 318
[28] G. Lentini, *Massimiliano Kolbe*, p.41.
[29] SK 486

This is the ascetical-mystical path of conversion and purification leading the soul to holiness. This is the spiritual journey during which the most intimate and complete transfiguration is by degrees accomplished through training the soul to continually model itself on the Immaculate. The soul must work with and through Her to effect the necessary detachment, renunciation and self-denial according to that fundamental norm of the Gospel spoken by Jesus Himself: *"If anyone wishes to come after Me, let him deny himself, and take up his cross, and follow Me"* (Mt 16:24) along the road which leads to the Kingdom of Heaven. This is what St. Maximilian repeatedly taught and wrote with his usual clarity: *"This is the tactic of the Immaculate: first Calvary, then Tabor. Glory to Her for everything."*[30]

In this way, the soul will practice the virtues heroically and exercise the gifts of the Holy Spirit with and through Her by an ever greater assimilation to Her. Moreover, through Her, in Her and like Her, the soul will live the life of Jesus according to the words of the Apostle, *"Have this mind in you which was also in Christ"* (Eph 2:5), so that *"the life also of Jesus may be made manifest in our mortal flesh"* (II Cor 4:11).

In summary, St. Louis M. Grignion de Montfort has already expressly written that "true devotion to Mary is *holy*, that is to say, it brings the soul to avoid sin and imitate the virtues of the Most Holy Virgin." Which virtues? The Saint responds by listing them in this manner: "Particularly Her profound humility, Her living faith, Her blind obedience, Her continual prayer, Her complete mortification, Her divine purity, Her ardent charity, Her heroic patience, Her angelic sweetness, and Her divine wisdom. These are the ten principle virtues of the Holy Virgin."[31]

We may also add to these ten principal virtues of Our Lady two more which are more typically "Franciscan," held most dear by our Seraphic Father St. Francis, namely: seraphic poverty and Franciscan joy.

Acquiring the virtues of the Immaculate means to clothe oneself with Her and, therefore, to resemble Her and assimilate oneself intimately to Her. St. Maximilian, in fact,

---

[30] SK 383
[31] *True Devotion*, n.108.

writes that the ideal *"is to become Hers ever more and more, in an ever more perfect manner, to make oneself more like unto Her, to become in a certain sense Her, so that She might take possession of our soul ever more completely, [so that She] might rule it totally and in and through it She Herself might think, speak, love God and neighbor, and act."*[32]

SHE GIVES BIRTH TO "JESUS" IN US

The Marian ascetical-mystical journey highlights in a specific way Mary's place and action in the development of the spiritual and supernatural life of those who have taken the *Marian Vow*. It highlights Her constant presence and action which increases and becomes ever more perfect. In both our personal and communal pursuit of holiness, the Immaculate, Spouse of the Holy Spirit, is present with the Holy Spirit as the active and effective cause of sanctity. She is present as the sublime teacher and brilliant model of our sanctification realized by authentic fidelity to the *Seraphic Rule*.

Indeed, She is the transcendent matrix of sanctity which is Jesus, the Word Incarnate. Those consecrated with the *Marian Vow* must reproduce Jesus in themselves, because She, and She alone, is the "mold of God"[33] as St. Augustine first called Her and later St. Louis de Montfort as well. She is, as it were, the "form" of Christ. She is the most perfect "matrix" who reproduces Jesus in all those who, through their consecration, give themselves to Her as Her "absolute property" and who are attentive and docile to Her maternal action of purification, illumination, and sanctification in their soul.

The most complete, perfect, and connatural christification of the soul comes, therefore, through and with its marianization. In fact Jesus was "made from Mary"—*factum ex muliere* (Gal 4:4)—from Her virginal flesh and blood by the working of the Holy Spirit. So we too desire mystically to be "made" from Mary, born of Her. We might even say that we desire to be "made" or formed, in a certain sense, from Her virginal flesh and blood by the action of the Holy Spirit. *"Behold we are thy bone and thy flesh"* (II Kings 5:1). This is what the Israelites said to King David and this is what we, too, want to be able to say to the Immaculate, our divine Mother Coredemptrix.

---

[32] SK 1211
[33] In Latin *forma Dei*.

Hence, it can truly be asserted that the Immaculate, in giving us birth, brings each of us forth precisely as another "Jesus." St. Louis de Montfort teaches that in consecrating oneself without limits to the Immaculate it can be said that the person *"has thrown himself into the very mold which formed Jesus."*[34] Thus, in making and living the *Marian Vow* it is *"natural"* that we become Jesus, that is to say that we become *"the natural portrait of Her divine Son,"*[35] since *"Mary Most Holy is the great cast of God prepared by the Holy Spirit in order to naturally form a God-Man by the hypostatic union and to form the man-God by grace."*[36] Therefore it will only be "natural" that *"whoever places himself in it and allows himself to be formed there immediately receives the features of Jesus Christ, true God."*[37]

If St. Paul was able to say that he *"was in labor"* in forming Christ in his spiritual children, how much more so can it be said of the Immaculate with Her superlative fullness of grace and Her motherhood through the working of the Holy Spirit! This is especially true for those who have professed the *Marian Vow* and live it out faithfully: *"My dear children, with whom I am in labor again, until Christ is formed in you!"* (Gal 4:19).

St. Maximilian succinctly writes: *"Every grace proceeds from the Father who eternally generates the Son… By means of this grace the Holy Spirit, who from all eternity proceeds from the Father and from the Son, forms souls in the Immaculate and through the Immaculate unto the likeness of the Firstborn, the God-Man."*[38] Precisely this is the primary value of being the "absolute property" of the Immaculate via the *Marian Vow* of unlimited consecration.

Indeed, the *Marian Vow* contains within itself the potential of christification through divine grace. This christification is accomplished by the work of the Holy Spirit and the Immaculate: it is accomplished by the action of the Holy Spirit who christifies the soul *"in the Immaculate and through the Immaculate."* The goal of the *Marian Vow*, therefore, is to manifest and actualize the most intimate reality of the soul christified *"in the Immaculate and through the Immaculate"* by the working of the Holy Spirit.

---

34 *True Devotion*, n.219.
35 Ibid., n.221
36 *The Secret of Mary*, n.17.
37 Ibid.
38 SK 1296

"EFFICIENT" AND "EXEMPLARY" CAUSE

Consequently, the Immaculate is called "efficient cause" and "exemplary cause" of our sanctification. She is, therefore, active and operative in bringing about the christification of the soul. She is by no means just a static, inert exemplar to be reproduced and nothing more. No, She is first and foremost an efficient cause who works in the first person in directly and concretely tending to the behavior of those who belong to Her.

Indeed, we know that, according to the teaching of St. Bonaventure, "there is no sanctification" without the presence and operation of the Immaculate. She Herself really conceives and brings us forth in Jesus so as to be "sons in the Son"—*Filii in Filio,* to summarize the Apostle Paul (cf. Rom 8:14–17, 29–30; Gal 4:6; Eph 1:3–5; cf. also Jn 1:12; I Jn 3:1). She always accompanies and assists each of Her children in Her own motherly way to pass through the ascending phases of the spiritual life, whether they are ascetical or mystical, until they reach the consummation of the intra-trinitarian life.

She is always operative as Mother throughout the entire journey of spiritual growth. This growth occurs along the *"Triple Way"* : *purgative, illuminative, unitive,* kindling that *incendium amoris*—that fire of love in the soul. St. Bonaventure expressly calls Her the *purgatrix, illuminatrix et perfectrix*.[39]

The teaching of St. Maximilian, in the school of St. Bonaventure, is clear-cut. He writes that the Immaculate *"penetrates our soul and directs its faculties with unlimited power. We truly belong to Her. Therefore, we are with Her always and everywhere…"*[40] If, therefore, we are truly Hers, then She can never leave us no matter what situation we may find ourselves in. Unfortunately, we are the ones who leave Her every time we are unfaithful to the *Marian Vow.*

St. Pio of Pietrelcina also spoke of this maternal presence of Our Lady in his faithful and fervent life of union with Her. With simplicity and assurance he was even able to write that *"My dear Mother*[41]*… is always with me."*[42]

> There are innumerable examples of Our Lady's activity in sanctifying souls which can be drawn from the lives of the

---

[39] *De Purificatione B.M.V.*, sermo I.
[40] SK 461
[41] *la Mammina* in Italian.
[42] *Epistolario*, vol. I, p.252.

Saints. Here we will limit ourselves to two examples, one from the life of St. Veronica Giuliani and the other from Venerable Fr. Gabriel Mary Allegra.

It can be said of St. Veronica Giuliani, especially in her later years, that she lived constantly under the gaze of Our Lady. She lived in such a way as to be led by Our Lady completely in her every action. *"If I begin working,"* writes the Saint, *"if I go to eat, if I go to take some rest, in all of my actions She is my guide and teacher. It seems to me that I always sense Her presence with me, that as a most faithful Mother, She may instruct me as to how to act in everything"* (from her *Diario*).

Regarding Ven. Fr. Gabriel let us read what he himself wrote to a confrere: *"I feel that I am always assisted by the Most Blessed Virgin in a visible manner, hence I would have to say that I am accustomed to being shipwrecked and being saved."* And in another letter he writes, *"I frequently sense that Our Lady is sweetly leading the little boat of my soul [...]. There is nothing else for me to do but abandon myself"* (from his *Vita*).

The Immaculate is the Mediatrix of every grace as the fruitful Spouse of the Holy Spirit, the Spouse of Him who is the Sanctifier; and He, as a matter of fact, never acts without His Spouse. This is what St. Maximilian teaches, following the school of St. Louis de Montfort. This latter maintains that he "who wants to enjoy the action of the Holy Spirit within himself must have His faithful and ever espoused Bride, the divine Mary."[43] Indeed, it is through Her motherhood and universal mediation of graces that the Immaculate, in synergy of spousal love with the Holy Spirit, has all graces at Her disposal and gives to Her consecrated children every necessary and abundant grace to begin, to grow, to be renewed, to be sustained, and to progress along the way of sanctification. These graces lead the soul into the bosom of the Most Holy Trinity so that the fatiguing and painful asceticism, accomplished with Her—the *Via Matris* alongside the *Via Crucis*—will be brought about in the easiest, briefest, and most fruitful way possible, as St. Louis de Montfort and St. Maximilian teach.

---

[43] *True Devotion*, c.4, a.5.

This asceticism realized with Her sanctifies the soul in such a way as to bring it to the very heights of perfection, namely of that most extraordinary grace of being like the Immaculate. This means the fullest and most perfect "conformity" to Jesus in the most intimate and burning union of love with the Sacred Hearts of Jesus and Mary: a burning love to be poured out, therefore, into all hearts and which must reign among all men, wherever they may be, and in all ages until the *Parousia*.

To those who frivolously consider union with Blessed Mary as an impediment to union with Jesus, St. Louis de Montfort—that great teacher of Marian devotion and consecration—responds with clarity: "Could it ever be possible that She, who found grace before God for everyone in general and for each in particular, might hinder a soul from finding the great grace of union with Jesus Christ? [...] The divine Mary, entirely lost in God, is not an obstacle in reaching divine union for perfect souls; to the contrary, as there has never been anyone in the past, so there shall never be anyone else in the future who can be more efficacious than Mary Most Holy in assisting us in this great work. This is true regarding the grace that She will communicate to us for this purpose [...] as well as the solicitude with which She will ever preserve us from the illusions and deceits of the evil one."[44]

RADICAL "UNLIMITEDNESS"

The radical condition necessary for this steep ascent of sanctification is *unlimitedness*. This, according to St. Maximilian, characterizes consecration to the Immaculate with its consequent self-abandonment and "loss of self" in Her hands.

As we know, with the *Marian Vow* we give not only our whole self to the Immaculate, but even all of our merits in the spiritual order and their reward so that She may freely dispose of them according to Her will. This renouncement and detachment also help in the "expropriation" of everything and in becoming ever more totally the "absolute property" of the Immaculate.

---

[44] *True Devotion*, n. 164–165.

Every offering of love and sorrow are included and present in this "unlimited" self-donation, without any sort of exclusion or exception. Thus, there is present the heroic offering of self as missionary in the lands of the infidels, including the most dangerous places in the world; the heroic offering of self as "victim" of expiation and reparation for the conversion and salvation of souls; the heroic offering of self even unto violent and bloody martyrdom (as happened in the case of St. Maximilian in Auschwitz).

If St. Bonaventure in his commentary on the *Seraphic Rule* was able to say that, according to the mind of St. Francis of Assisi, *"those who are received into our Order must be disposed for martyrdom,"*[45] then how much more must every Franciscan with the *Marian Vow* be disposed for martyrdom.

We find ourselves here at the heights of full love to be realized in complete dedication and total self-immolation. We are speaking about the summit of love longing to give one's life and blood without reserve; we are speaking about that summit of love which Jesus scultped with His divine words, *"Greater love than this no one has, that one lay down his life for his friends"* (Jn 15:13).

So it is that the Immaculate, through the *Marian Vow*, desires to bring us to live this unlimited and supreme love. In this sense the *Marian Vow* can rightly be called the vow of unlimited love, of that love which does not stop even in the face of death, but bears up, defeats and overcomes it. Such love disposes us even for violent martyrdom consequent on persecutions; it disposes us for missionary sacrifice which may consume us in the lands of the infidels; it disposes us to be "victims" offered and sacrificed as saving hosts.

One has only to call to mind the various inspiring "chapters" of the *Marian Vow* "written" by the lives of our Patrons:

> - The chapter on St. Francis' bloody stigmatization on Monte la Verna, where he became a true crucifix under the eyes of the Madonna and his death at the *"Portiuncula,"* dedicated to St. Mary of the Angels;

> - The chapter on St. Clare's death after twenty-eight years of sickness which kept her bedridden and consumed her day after day on her austere straw bed at the convent of San Damiano in Assisi;

---

[45] Cf. *Expositio super Regulam*, 2.

- The chapter on the heroic, voluntary death of St. Maximilian, the martyr and "fool of the Immaculate," who gave his life in the horrible starvation bunker as a substitute for the father of a family condemned to death in Auschwitz;

- The chapter on the death of St. Pio of Pietrelcina, a lover of the Rosary, who lived for fifty years at Galgano as a bleeding victim bearing the stigmata, and whose victimhood was consummated in his daily ministering of the Sacrament of Confession for the salvation of souls.

These are chapters on the *Marian Vow* realizing unlimited love for the Immaculate to be translated into love for God and the brethren by way of a most perfect identification with Jesus Crucified. This conformity to Christ is the most precious fruit of the life that is entirely seraphic and Marian.

There are two very interesting points in the thought of St. Maximilian which should be kept in mind because of their convincing and salutary radicalism.

The first regards the terminology St. Maximilian uses in regard to consecrating, donating and giving oneself in love to the Immaculate. His terminology implicitly includes every expression of self-offering that will be or might possibly be used in the future. These more radical expressions to be discovered or devised in the future, he writes, are already included in the consecration: *"If, then, others may find expressions signifying an even greater sacrifice and oblation of self,"*[46] these are already included in our consecration. St. Maximilian was already intent on placing no reservations. He writes, *"These are beautiful expressions: servant, son, slave, possession, property; but we desire even more, we want to be Hers without any limitation, thus including all of these meanings and any others that shall be invented or which could still be invented."*[47]

The second regards the request which St. Maximilian makes of the Immaculate that She might rule over those

---
[46] SK 508
[47] SK 508; cf. also SK 1211

consecrated to Her without any regard for their personal preferences, even to the point of being *tyrannical* and *despotic* towards them. He writes, *"We are consecrated to Her unlimitedly, hence we do not have rights over our thoughts, our actions or our words. May She rule over us* 'despotically.' *May She benevolently deign to pay no respect to our free will and, if we should desire to unfetter ourselves from Her immaculate hand, may She* constrain *us, even if this would cause us to suffer greatly, even if we were to protest or refuse or beg otherwise; may She pay attention to none of it, rather may She constrain us with force and, in that very moment, clasp us to Her Heart even more strongly."*[48]

LOVE OF THE "PIERCED" HEART

Furthermore, we can view the vows in reference to the most meaningful symbols of Christ's Passion. If the other three religious vows of obedience, poverty, and chastity are symbolized, according to spiritual tradition, by the three nails which made Jesus "Love Crucified," the *Marian Vow* comes instead to be symbolized by that *"lance"* which pierced the Heart of Jesus on the Cross (cf. Jn 19:34), and which likened to a *"sword"* pierced the divine Mother and Coredemptrix at the foot of the Cross, according to the prophecy of the aged Simeon at the Presentation of the Child Jesus in the Temple of Jerusalem (cf. Lk 2:35).

Hence, the *Marian Vow* may be said to have had its full realization precisely on Calvary. Indeed, it is right and holy to think that the *Marian Vow* gushes forth from the pierced Hearts of Christ and Mary. The words spoken by Jesus Crucified to His Mother, *"Woman, behold thy Son,"* and to His beloved disciple, *"Behold thy Mother"* (Jn 19:26–27), followed shortly after by the death of Jesus, were sealed by the lance of Longinus, opening the Heart of the Crucified Redeemer and entirely transfixing the Heart of the Mother Coredemptrix (cf. Jn 19:34).

It was the surge of redemptive love, therefore, which opened the Hearts of Jesus and Mary in that torrential outpouring of every gift of love. This surge of divine love and torrential outpouring of every gift of divine love of the Hearts of Jesus and Mary are the

---
[48] SK 373

content of the *Marian Vow* in its fullness. The *Marian Vow*, in fact, is well-rooted in and expressed by these two sayings of Jesus: *"Love one another;...as I have love you, you also love one another"* (Jn 13:34) and *"Greater love than this no one has: that one lay down his life for his friends"* (Jn 15:13).

Anyone, therefore, who reflects deeply upon the *Marian Vow* can readily grasp how it is a treasure of love: that is to say, a treasure of inestimable worth which adorns and enriches all the virtues through unlimited love and, in a particular manner, a treasure which enhances the three vows of religion as well as the whole of Franciscan religious life. We shall see the influence of the *Marian Vow* upon the other vows of religious life after we briefly reflect upon the "mission" of the *Marian Vow* and the living "presence" of the Immaculate which accompanies it.

CHAPTER 3
THE MISSION OF THE MARIAN VOW

The "mission" of the *Marian Vow* of unlimited consecration to the Immaculate is nothing less than the very mission of the Immaculate Mediatrix Herself. In other words, the *Marian Vow* lived out generously and faithfully through perfect observance of the *Book of Sanctification*, will transform the Franciscan Friar or Sister of the Immaculate into the Immaculate Mediatrix of divine grace who then must be given to all mankind in need of salvation.

TO BE TRANSFIGURED INTO THE IMMACULATE

The consecrated person must be transfigured into the person of the Immaculate by living the vow of unlimited dedication to the Immaculate in its profundity and totality. St. Maximilian M. Kolbe expressed this with the bold term of *transubstantiation* into the Immaculate in order to realize the most complete *"conformity"* to Jesus (cf. Rm 8:29).

This means that every Franciscan with the *Marian Vow* is called and must exert himself so as to live an "immaculate" life which is all grace and no sin, all virtue and no vice, all radiance and no shadows. In a word, we are speaking of a heavenly life, not earthly, which is capable of making us, as St. Maximilian writes, *"ever more like the Immaculate…ever more—like Her—immaculate."*[49]

Great is the responsibility of every Franciscan with the *Marian Vow*, therefore. He must be *immaculateness* itself: immaculate in his entirely pure life, immaculate within so as to be radical and complete in rejecting sin, living a life rich and radiant in its fullness of grace.

As such, this immaculateness not only excludes every impurity of thought, heart, and body, but excludes any stain, any moral deformity of any kind, even minimal. It excavates even the

---
[49] SK 757

most intimate part of the soul and arrives at purifying even the subterraneous meanderings and deepest secrets of the *ego* in order to liberate it from self-centeredness which stands at the root of our self-love and from which flows the search for self-satisfaction and self-affirmation through every defect and sin that is committed.

To know the Immaculate, therefore, is of primary importance in order to love and imitate Her, to praise and glorify Her. Knowledge of the Immaculate is essential in order to gaze upon Her virtues and mirror them in our life, in order to keep Her always present and remain always present to Her by staying very close to Her Heart. St. Maximilian writes with great fervor: *"May She drag all of us to Herself by the hand and press us to Her Immaculate Heart, and each one of us individually, in such wise that we have not the capacity and cannot detach ourselves from Her."*[50]

St. Maximilian is rightly regarded as having produced a prolific quantity of writings about the reality of transfiguration and transformation into the Immaculate. So it would not be difficult here to put together a little anthology of quotes on this theme. Here we shall limit ourselves to but a few texts from among the most important of the relevant passages, besides those already reported throughout the present work.

"The essence [...] is unlimited consecration to the Immaculate [...] We must belong to Her under every aspect; we must be Hers in the strictest and most perfect way possible; we must be, in a certain sense, She Herself."[51]

"The essence [...] is to annihilate oneself and become Her. The fundamental element of such a transformation consists in conforming, fusing, unifying our will with Hers."[52]

"Let us disappear in Her! May She alone remain, and we in Her, a part of Her. But is it licit for us [...] to rave in this manner? Nonetheless, this is the truth, the reality."[53]

---

[50] SK 463
[51] SK 634, 1210
[52] SK 579
[53] SK 461

> "We are Hers, of the Immaculate, unlimitedly Hers, perfectly Hers; we are, as it were, Her very self. She, by means of us, loves the good God. She, with our poor heart, loves Her divine Son. We become the means by which the Immaculate loves Jesus, and Jesus, seeing that we are Her property, a part, as it were, of His most loving Mother, loves Her in and through us. What beautiful mysteries!"[54]

MEDITATING SO AS TO ASSIMILATE THE IMMACULATE

From all of this comes the need to study and, even more importantly, of daily meditation upon the mystery of Mary, to be unveiled and pondered in-depth without let-up or slow down. This is important because only through a meditation which advances towards the highest contemplation can we arrive at repeating with true conviction, *de Maria numquam satis* ("of Mary never enough"). We must repeat this saying of St. Bernard. In his teachings St. Maximilian informs and admonishes us that the Immaculate is not only not well-known as of yet, but that She is not even little-known yet![55]

To speak of study, meditation, and contemplation means to speak of concentration and interiority requiring a life of "silence" in a religious house. St. Maximilian teaches this when he says: *"When there is silence, there is also interior recollection; and when there is recollection, there is also prayer; and when there is prayer, there is also the fulfillment of God's will through love; and therefore there is holiness."*[56]

> And it is instructive, as well as edifying, to recall the little episode of St. Maximilian with a confrere on the evening of November 8th, 1940 (nine months before his martyrdom!) in the infirmary of the friary. The Saint had gone there to take some medicine and a confrere struck up a conversation. The colloquy extended even past nine o'clock, that is, even during the time of "rigorous silence" established by the rule of the community.

---

[54] SK 508
[55] Cf. SK 1242
[56] Cf. G. Lentini, *Massimiliano Kolbe*, p. 311.

The next day Fr. Maximilian sent a note to the confrere with which he had spoken the prior evening with the following message: *"Dear Father! I beg you to forgive me for the scandal I gave last evening after 9 pm in the infirmary, behaving as if, in that moment, there was not in effect the rigorous silence."*[57]

What is most admirable about that note? St. Maximilian's humility? His fidelity to perfect common observance of the life? His great love for silence? His spirit of reparation for a transgression committed? This is the school of the Saints that we must make our own.

For study, meditation and contemplation to be fruitful, it goes without saying that there cannot be lacking that element of loving penance and mortification. This element is necessary for basic Christian life; it is indispensable for crucifying the *"flesh with its passions and desires"* (Gal 5:24), for dominating the impulses and cravings of the flesh *"which war against the soul"* (1 Pt 2:11), for keeping and offering the body *"as a sacrifice, living, holy, pleasing to God"* (Rm 12:1) to the point of making it *hostiam puram, hostiam sanctam, hostiam immaculatam* ("a pure, holy and unblemished sacrifice"—Roman Canon, Euch. Prayer I).

The Immaculate is without any shadow of sin; She is full of grace; She is entirely divine love; She is entirely of God; She is "all Jesus," "all Holy Spirit" and simultaneously "very human." Therefore, to be transfigured into Her means to live a Christian life that is "human," true, but also a life which is entirely graced by God and utterly humble and poor, totally aflame with faith, hope and charity, all virginally pure, abounding in prayer and mortification, ruled *in toto* by love of God and neighbor.

The *Marian Vow*, therefore, ought to keep each Franciscan of the Immaculate far away from "mediocrity" so as to carry him ever higher and higher to the most perfect likeness of the Immaculate. This perfect resemblance with the Immaculate becomes an identification with Her as occurred with St. Clare of Assisi[58] and gives the friar or sister the "face of Mary," the face of Her, that is to say, whose "face most resembles Christ," as Dante Alighieri says in speaking of the "face" of the Madonna.[59] Indeed, it is only in the Immaculate

---

[57] SK 920
[58] Cf. (St. Clare) *Process of Canonization* (FF 3083).
[59] *Paradiso*, XXXII, 85–86.

that the most sublime "conformity" to Jesus (cf. Rm 8:29) can be accomplished, that *conformity-to-Christ* which is most complete, perfect, and loving.

TRANSFIGURATION INTO THE MEDIATRIX

What is more, the mission of the *Marian Vow* reaches out to others in the apostolate. It is decisively directed towards our brothers in exile and is intent upon saving and sanctifying souls—and it cannot be otherwise. In writing about those consecrated without limits to the Immaculate, St. Maximilian brilliantly expressed his thought: *"Jesus Christ is the only Mediator between God and mankind; the Immaculate is the only Mediatrix between Jesus and mankind; and we shall be the happy mediators between the Immaculate and the souls dispersed throughout the world."*[60]

That is not all. It can also be said that the Franciscan with the *Marian Vow* has the primary task of transfiguring himself into the Immaculate with the precise goal of carrying forward the very mission of the Immaculate *Mediatrix of grace and salvation*. It could be said that it is not he that acts, but rather the Immaculate is setting him in motion and operating as the universal Mediatrix in action in order to give salvation to humanity by giving birth to Jesus "in the hearts of the faithful by means of the Church" (LG 65).

Here the reflection again to focus on the causal relation between being and acting in the Immaculate Mediatrix, a relation which should emerge in the life of each Franciscan of the Immaculate (and of anyone who professes our *Marian Vow*). We can say that in every Franciscan with the *Marian Vow* the *being* of the Immaculate and, consequently, the *action* of the Mediatrix must be perceptible. We can also say that the Immaculate is She who, within the consecrated soul, *"is"* present in Her essential fullness of grace; whereas the Mediatrix is She who *acts* through that soul in virtue of Her dynamic fruitfulness of grace, one which She distributes and desires to see spread and active in all men in need of salvation and each person in particular.

All of this must be seen in relation to the mystery of the Church. There is a celestial interaction between the saving action of the Immaculate who gives birth to Jesus "in the hearts of the faithful by means of the Church" (LG 65) and the saving action of the Church which "gives birth to a new and immortal life in her

---

[60] SK 577

children" (LG 64). The Church, in fact, brings forth the life of grace and the Immaculate is the Mother of that grace.

As universal Coredemptrix in harmonious dependence and union with the one Redeemer, the field of action for Her saving, maternal mediation is the whole of humanity to be snatched from Satan, conquered for the Kingdom of God, and brought to the Heart of Christ through grace. This has to be accomplished through the Church by means of the work of evangelization and the action of the Sacraments. The Church must be and shall always be active *"even to the very ends of the earth"* (Acts 1:8).

In a brief, but dense text, Pope John Paul II in *Redemptoris Mater* brilliantly explains the strict relationship between Mary, with Her mediation and maternal action, and the Church. He writes, "With Her new motherhood in the Spirit, Mary embraces everyone and each person in particular *in the Church;* She also embraces everyone and each person in particular *through* the Church" (RM 47).

This is the saving mission of the universal Immaculate Mediatrix. This, therefore, is our apostolic mission, we who are consecrated to the Immaculate Mediatrix through the *Marian Vow*. This means that our field of action is the whole of mankind in need of salvation. Consequently, it is our duty to remain in the immaculate hands of the universal Mediatrix, to be Her docile instruments, to allow ourselves to be carried and placed wherever She wishes, and to labor in every place and continent on the planet, wherever She chooses and as She chooses in accord with God's saving design which She knows so well.

THE MISSIONARY CHARACTER OF THE MARIAN VOW

This is the missionary vocation, or better, the missionary character and zeal contained in the *Marian Vow* which is truly global in scope and which is proper to all of us who have taken the *Marian Vow*. Hence, it could also be said that all of the Franciscan Friars or Sisters of the Immaculate, the Poor Clares of the Immaculate, as well as the members of the Mission of the Immaculate Mediatrix (M.I.M.) who have taken the *Marian Vow,* must reproduce in themselves the

Immaculate Mediatrix, namely, She who is the universal *missionary* and *evangelist*.

"Divine inspiration"

In chapter twelve of the *Seraphic Rule*, St. Francis of Assisi spoke to the friars of "those who, by divine inspiration, wish to go among the Saracens and other infidels." We can also say that here he intended to speak specifically to the Franciscans of the Immaculate who have the gift of the missionary vocation by virtue of the *Marian Vow*. As a matter of fact, it is precisely the *Marian Vow* which contains within itself that authentic, missionary, and "divine inspiration" completely intact. St. Maximilian, inspired by the example of our Seraphic Father, writes, *"Our Father St. Francis is the model missionary; his example and Rule are highly missionary and allow for the maximum apostolic zeal directed towards the salvation and sanctification of souls."*[61]

The "most perfect" obedience

When St. Francis speaks of that obedience which is "more perfect than any other,"[62] or of the "highest obedience,"[63] namely to want to go to the missions *ad Gentes*, it could be said that he intends again to speak, or speaks by way of anticipation, of the Franciscans of the Immaculate who are entirely disposed and ready to be sent at any given moment to the mission lands, wherever they may be.

Here, in fact, is the most valid and probing *test* of our vocation as Franciscans of the Immaculate. The Franciscan Friar or Sister of the Immaculate who is not ready to go to any mission whatsoever cannot make the *Marian Vow* and, therefore, does not have the vocation to be a Franciscan of the Immaculate.

No "buts," no "reservations"

It must be well understood that this *missionary character*, with its "unlimited" love for souls in need of salvation, cannot allow for any reservation or impediment. If we are called to go here or to

---
[61] SK 299
[62] Celano, *Second Life of St. Francis of Assisi*, 152 (FF 736).
[63] *Mirror of Perfection*, 48 (FF 1736).

go there, even when there is the certain risk of losing our life as St. Maximilian teaches us, there cannot be any "buts" or "ifs."

St. Maximilian writes that those consecrated with the *Marian Vow* must love souls in such a way that they are disposed *"to go, for the sake of the Immaculate, wherever holy obedience shall send them, even if it means going to the toughest missions and that meeting up with death is sure."*[64] *"For the sake of the Immaculate,"* they must *"be ready to go wherever and whenever the Superiors shall send them, without regard for the difficulties and dangers."*[65]

Heroism…without limits

This, clearly, is heroic. However, the *Marian Vow* is precisely a vow which demands heroism; it requires *"action of a heroic character and perfection without limits,"* as St. Maximilian writes.[66] Hence, it is not for everyone; rather it is only for the Immaculate's "dearly beloved." It is for those who have been chosen and called to the sublime mission of being transfigured into Her, the Immaculate Lady full of grace and holiness; to those called to be transfigured into Her, the Mediatrix of all grace who works for the salvation of all mankind in the world; to those called to bring Her everywhere in order to give Her to all. *"She needs to be brought into all hearts,"* declares St. Maximilian, *"so that She, upon entering into these hearts, may give birth there to the sweet Jesus, to God, and bring Him up even to that perfect age. What a beautiful mission!"*[67]

> Historically, it is known how St. Francis of Assisi had the hope of dying a martyr and three times went out as a missionary to the Middle East.[68] Holy Mother Clare of Assisi also wanted to leave and to be a missionary among the infidels of Morocco and to die a martyr.[69]

> St. Maximilian can literally be said to have burned with missionary zeal in order to bring the Immaculate to all hearts. He was able to go to Japan where he founded the City of

---

[64] SK 399
[65] SK 402
[66] SK 1272
[67] SK 508
[68] Cf. Bonaventure, *Legenda Minor*, Ch. 3, L. IX; Celano, *First Life of St. Francis of Assisi*, Ch. 20, 55 & 56 (FF 1356, 417–420, 422).
[69] Cf. (St. Clare) *Process of Canonization* (FF 3029, 3042).

the Immaculate *Mugenzai No Sono*. But he also went to India where he was already preparing to place a community of friars; and he went to China, and to Latvia, and then to Beirut… In a word, he hoped to arrive everywhere in order to invade the world with the Immaculate. With this in mind he even envisioned preparations for an airfield to be located in *Niepokalanòw* in Poland.

Whenever someone would ask St. Maximilian how big the cemetery should be in *Niepokalanòw*, he would give this meaningful response: *"I am of the opinion that a large area of land would not be necessary for the cemetery of the Niepokalanòw in Poland since most of the bones of its inhabitants will be laid to rest in the most varied parts of the earth. We shall embrace the whole world!"*[70]

Nor should it be forgotten that St. Pio of Pietrelcina himself, as a young friar, was inspired to ask for a missionary obedience to go to the Indies, even though it was not granted him by his superiors due to his precarious health.

Hence, all the friars and sisters with the *Marian Vow*, wherever they may be found, must be a living and active presence of the Immaculate Mediatrix. They must carry the Immaculate with them and give Her to everyone. They must make Her known and loved and bring Her, as St. Maximilian says, *"into every heart that beats upon the earth."* This is because it is Her mission to "restore supernatural life to souls," as Vatican II teaches (LG 61). The Immaculate Mediatrix alone is the one who gives birth to Jesus in hearts; She is the one who, as the Mother of divine grace, regenerates souls in need of salvation and sanctification in the Church. She accomplishes this mission throughout all time and space until the universal *eschaton*.

It is essential that the entire fraternal life of the religious communities with the *Marian Vow* be animated and leavened by this missionary ideal. The members of the community, both individually and as a whole, must be committed to binding themselves to the universal Immaculate Mediatrix. In this way they will find themselves more united and close-knit in their missionary efforts for the salvation and sanctification of all souls in every part of the world.

---

[70] SK 404

St. Maximilian writes that *"the more each one of us draws near to the Immaculate, the more we will draw near to one another through the Immaculate, and in this unity lies our strength."*[71] This is our strength for evangelizing all the continents in the world, and especially the most vast continent of Asia, so that it can have *"the possibility of knowing Jesus Christ by means of the Immaculate and in order to bring Heaven closer to mankind."*[72]

His first apostolic project which he employed, not only on the national level, but even internationally, was that of the *Marian press*. It was his desire to *"envelope the entire earth"* with Marian publications in order to present the Immaculate to every person and introduce into the heart of everyone She who is the Mother of the Savior.

But in order to accomplish all of this it is obvious that not just any type of loving fervor for the Immaculate will do; an ordinary dedication to the apostolate is just not sufficient. Rather, exceptional fervor and commitment are necessary, a fervor and commitment of the "mad," such as St. Maximilian asked of a confrere, fra Mariano Wòjcik, to dedicate to a project for a huge increase in the already large press run of The *Knight of the Immaculate* and for founding a *City of the Immaculate* in China and Japan.

These are St. Maximilian's words: *"Fra Mariano, write me also at Niepokalanòw whether you still intend to persevere in your intention of dedicating yourself to the work of the Immaculate, whether you really want to consecrate your entire life to Her and wear yourself out completely, whether you are disposed to accept the possibility of even shortening your very existence as a result of hunger and hardships and to expose yourself to a premature death for the Immaculate.*

"Write me at Niepokalanòw so that—in view of the fact that we are about to open up new outposts for the 'Knight' and to initiate the M.I. in other nations—I might make an actual numerical count of the—as we like to say—madmen available among us for this cause."[73]

---

[71] SK 571
[72] SK 758
[73] SK 228

The generous effort on the part of the friars to study and learn the languages most spoken in the world must be of particular importance. It is a necessary and very important effort, this one, and it must be done in order to make our own the apostolic and missionary commitment of St. Maximilian. He writes: *"We desire to speak to every soul that is living on this earth and in every language [...]. With the passing of time, we do not want to transgress even one of the more common languages spoken in the world."*[74]

Poverty, sacrifice, fervor, and ardor must concretely characterize the Franciscan of the Immaculate with the *Marian Vow* who is dedicated to the apostolate of the Marian press. This is how St. Maximilian spontaneously described the friar of *Niepokalanòw*: *"What is a friar of Niepokalanòw? Behold him: he is one who, with a bundle of publications under his arm, climbs onto an airplane of the latest model and flies there, where it is necessary to save souls."*[75]

---

[74] SK 880
[75] Reported by G. Lentini, *Massimiliano Kolbe*, p. 265.

CHAPTER 4
THE MARIAN VOW: "PRESENCE" OF THE IMMACULATE

In the school of St. Maximilian we learn that unlimited consecration to the Immaculate, lived out in its fullness, brings us to the mystical transubstantiation into the Immaculate. This analogy of the Saint recalls the transubstantiation of the Eucharist where the Host and Wine, once consecrated, retain only their "species" or the "appearance" of bread and wine, whereas their "substance" is transmuted into the Body, Blood, Soul, and Divinity of Jesus.

This means that the *Marian Vow* fully lived out brings about, by way of analogy, the "loss" and complete "annihilation" of self. As a consequence, it can be said that the Immaculate lives mystically in us while we always retain our human "appearance." In the end *"She alone"* remains, as St. Maximilian so succinctly puts it.[76]

Furthermore, the potential of unlimited consecration to the Immaculate multiplies with the *Marian Vow*. This is so by virtue of the very grace of the *"vow"* which binds the soul to the Immaculate with the most sacred and indissoluble religious bond possible. Thus, the *Marian Vow* renders us entirely Her "property," marking and sealing us, in a certain sense, as Her *"absolute property,"* according to the exact expression of St. Maximilian.[77]

What stands out here is the fact that the living presence of the Immaculate in us gradually acquires a consistency which, when actualized in its totality and fullness, cannot be anything less than a dominating force. This presence of the Immaculate, fully actualized, truly carries the soul to the summit of sanctity and perfection, namely, the participation in the very holiness and unequalled perfection of the Immaculate.

---

[76] Cf. SK 461
[77] SK 1160

Indeed, it is sufficient to recall that the concrete unlimitedness of our dedication and belonging to the Immaculate which renders us Her *"absolute property"* leads us to that transubstantiation into Her. As a result of this, behind the intact appearance of our humanity, there remains solely the Immaculate; in reality *"She alone"* remains with an exclusive presence.

The most concrete and expressive image of this reality, which is totally spiritual, is that of the mother. She carries the child in her womb and in the first months of gestation there is no noticeable change exteriorly. She possesses and forms him in the secret place of her womb while the child who is present lives through, with, and for her alone. The mother, in reality, is his entire life, his entire substance, since she is giving to him her flesh and blood.

MARIAN "TRANSUBSTANTIATION" AND THE EUCHARISTIC LIFE

The specific term "transubstantiation" recalls the ineffable mystery of the Eucharist in a striking way and directly refers to it by way of analogy. We all are well aware that at the Consecration of the Bread and Wine during the Holy Sacrifice of the Mass, Jesus, living and true, is really present behind the unchanged and intact appearances of bread and wine with His Body and Blood, Soul and Divinity.

The reference and analogy to the Eucharist on the part of St. Maximilian is truly audacious and amazing. Thus, the potential of grace in the *Marian Vow* for those who correspond more and more to being modeled upon Her, effects an assimilation to Her and hence their transformation into the Immaculate. Such a transformation can reach the point where, behind the human appearances, solely the Immaculate really remains, precisely *"She* alone*"* remains, as St. Maximilian expressly states.

But if the Immaculate is the human person who is so utterly conformed to Christ and christified, if She is such a perfect bearer of Christ and light of Christ,[78] then it follows that those with the *Marian Vow*, by uniting themselves to the Immaculate, can reach the point of being totally assimilated in and transubstantiated into Her. It can be said, therefore, that each of them becomes utterly

---

[78] Successively *Cristiforme, Cristificata, Cristifera,* and *Cristifora* in Italian.

conformed to Christ and christified, a perfect bearer of Christ and light of Christ.[79]

It does not take much reflection to grasp that Marian transubstantiation and Eucharistic transubstantiation form a unity, just as the Immaculate and the Eucharist are united *ab imis*, that is to say, in their source. The Immaculate and the Eucharist, as a matter of fact, form a unity at the indivisible source in the sense that the consecrated Host, at its root, is the supersubstantial Bread made from the immaculate flesh of the ever Virgin Mary, and the consecrated Wine is, at its root, the virginal Blood of Mary's motherly Heart.

Who shall ever be able to separate the Eucharist from the Immaculate? If the *Marian Vow* assimilates us into the Immaculate, how could we ever live the *Marian Vow* without having a truly intense and eminent Eucharistic life?

Actually, one could say that to be transubstantiated into the Immaculate in a certain sense means to be transubstantiated into the Eucharist, and vice versa. No one, in fact, shall be able to live out the Eucharist as profoundly as those who are transubstantiated into the Immaculate; and no one shall be able to live out the mystery of the Immaculate as profoundly as those who allow themselves to be transubstantiated by the Eucharist and into the Eucharist.

Consequently, it is of primary importance that the Eucharistic life necessarily blossom forth as the most beautiful and fragrant flower[80] of transubstantiation into the Immaculate. In living according to the *Marian Vow*, therefore, we must produce this most exquisite flower of the Eucharistic life both as a result of being transubstantiated into the Immaculate and transubstantiated into the Eucharist Itself.

> By reflecting more in-depth on the subject according to the thought of St. Maximilian, one can readily comprehend the solid consistency of the Eucharistic life, especially in relation to the *Marian Vow*. As we all know from his biography, the rich patrimony of St. Maximilian's totally Marian and seraphic life was, in fact, his example: Eucharistic adoration during the day, numerous Visits to the Blessed Sacrament by day and night, continual spiritual Communions, and acts of adoring love towards the Eucharist.

---

[79] Successively *cristiforme, cristificato, cristiforo,* and *cristifero* in Italian.
[80] *fior fiore* in Italian.

St. Maximilian recommended in a special way receiving daily Eucharistic Communion in union with Our Lady, and specifically by having Her prepare the soul for Holy Communion. *"There is no better preparation for Holy Communion,"* he writes, *"than to offer it totally to the Immaculate (doing for our part, of course, all that we can). She will prepare our heart in the best of ways and we can thus be certain to procure the greatest joy and to manifest the greatest love for Jesus."*[81]

Indeed, we can say that this union with the Eucharistic Jesus both sacramentally and spiritually brings about the fullest presence of the Immaculate in those who live the *Marian Vow* in its totality. Venerable Olier actually speaks of Mary's presence in the soul as a *sacramental* reality, in a certain sense, because She is, as it were, a *"sacrament"* through which Jesus communicates His divine life to the soul.[82]

Everyone with the *Marian Vow* is called in a particular way to live and cultivate this most precious "presence" of the Immaculate. It is a spiritual, but real presence; a mystical, yet concrete presence; a presence which becomes a constant inseparability from Her by day and by night, in prayer and in work, when reposing and when working, in times of joy and in times of pain. The Saints who were especially bound to Our Lady experienced this and taught others about it, starting with St. Joseph, Spouse of the Immaculate, and continuing with all the Saints who were more committed to loving Her and making Her loved.

We are dealing here with a "presence," in reality, which could also be said to be "analogous" or "similar" to the presence of the Most Holy Trinity indwelling in the soul. Fr. Ragazzini writes with clarity in this regard, "On the plane of mystical experiences it seems that there may be something *similar* to what Theology asserts regarding the presence of the Most Holy Trinity in the soul by means of *indwelling*."[83] Here we want to pause and take in, even if only briefly, at least some additional rays of light and love regarding this presence.

---

[81] SK 643
[82] *Autobiografia*, 161.
[83] *Maria vita dell'anima*, p.228.

CHAPTER 4
A PRESENCE "ANALOGOUS" TO THAT OF THE MOST HOLY TRINITY IN THE SOUL IN THE STATE OF GRACE

For those consecrated with the *Marian Vow*, the presence of Mary can be considered "analogous" or "similar" to the presence of the Most Holy Trinity in the soul in the state of grace. This can be understood by the affirmation of Bl. William Chaminade who writes, *"There is a gift of the habitual presence of the most Holy Virgin, just as there is a gift of the habitual presence of God."*

Mary's presence is a *mystical* presence, that is to say mysterious and invisible; but at the same time it is a *real* presence, that is to say a maternal presence of Mary's person in soul and body. In other words, it is a presence which realizes a "physical-mystical union by the physical-mystical participation in the life of grace of Christ and Mary," as Fr. Ragazzini explains.[84] As She is in Heaven, so it could be said that the Immaculate is personally present before, beside, and within my soul which is upon the earth.

This personal presence of Mary, obviously, is not, nor could it ever be, infinite or on a par with the *infinite ubiquity of God*, because the Blessed Virgin Mary is always a finite creature. Nonetheless, it is certainly an exceptional presence and, one could say, incommensurable. This is because, with Her motherhood which gives birth to and embraces the whole human race and the entire Mystical Body (Head and Body), Her presence extends to all. Her presence is united with that of the special presence of the Eucharistic Jesus in every consecrated Host, a presence which transcends the limits of time and space.

If Her motherhood is real and personal, then this means that Mary's person must actually be near to each child She has borne and nourished as Mother. This began with Her *"Firstborn,"* Jesus, and continues for all of the *"many brethren"* of that *"Firstborn"* (Rm 8:29), including he who shall be the last-born at the end of time.

Truly it is unthinkable that Mary's motherhood towards Her children be only on the cognitive or affective level, that it be a presence bestowing grace merely *in distans* (at a distance). *Operatio sequitur esse* (work/activity is consequent on being) is an irrefutable principle. The experiences of the Saints in this regard are very concrete and enlightening. Here it is sufficient to recall two life experiences: one of St. Veronica Giuliani, and the other of St. Pio of Pietrelcina.

---

[84] *Maria vita dell'anima*, p. 243.

St. Veronica Giuliani writes, with her usual simplicity, "*The Most Holy Virgin... gave me a tender embrace, placed my head upon Her bosom and my soul was rapt into ecstasy.*"[85] The entire diary of this extraordinary Saint is filled with episodes like this.

St. Pio of Pietrelcina recounts that one day, having Our Lady at his side, it seemed to him as if She truly "*had nothing else to think about but me alone, filling my heart with holy affections.*"[86] He maintained that it was Our Lady who brought penitents to him, taking them "by the hand."[87]

It must be reaffirmed, therefore, that Mary's motherhood by the grace of the omnipotent God is a transcendent motherhood inserted into the order of the hypostatic union. Hence, as Mother, She is entirely capable of embracing and keeping close to Herself the whole of humanity as an only child pressed close to Her Heart! Moreover, each child cannot live nor think differently about the real, personal relationship with his own dear Mother.

In this regard the teaching of the Supreme Pontiff and Servant of God John Paul II is splendid. In his encyclical *Redemptoris Mater*, n. 45, he writes, "The fact of referring oneself to the person is an essential of motherhood. Motherhood always determines a *unique and unrepeatable relationship* between two persons: between the mother and the son, between the son and the mother."[88]

As a result, the assertion is true which says that in every Eucharistic Tabernacle, in every consecrated Host, and wherever Jesus the Son is present, His Mother Mary is also mystically present. It cannot be otherwise.

A significant and striking image of the Gospel comes to mind here; it is an image Jesus adopts in presenting Himself as the Savior of mankind, namely, the image of the hen who, under her wings, holds tight each one of her little chicks in order to protect and guard them: "*Jerusalem, Jerusalem!... How often would I have gathered thy children together, as a hen gathers her young under her wings...*" (Mt 23:37).

---

[85] Cf. *Diario*, p. 227.
[86] Cf. *Epistolario*, vol. I, Letter of May 6, 1913.
[87] M. Iasenza Niro, *Padre Pio parla della Madonna*, p.92.
[88] Cf. also Bl. John Duns Scotus, *In III Sententiarum*, d. 9.

LIVING THIS "PRESENCE"

There are abundant confirmations of this personal and active "presence" of the Immaculate in the lives of the Saints throughout the two-millennial history of the Church. Many of these Saints even had *mystical experiences* of this "presence," for example: St. Charles of Sezze, St. Maximilian M. Kolbe, St. Pio of Pietrelcina, and Ven. Fr. Gabriel Mary Allegra. Their edifying biographies overflow with this "presence" which thoroughly sanctified their heroic virtues with grace.

As a matter of fact, in the writings of the Church Fathers during the first centuries of the Church we find enlightening instruction from several Fathers who speak of this "presence" and the life of union with Our Lady in explicit and concrete terms.

Reference has already been made earlier to the thought of St. Ephrem (†373). This great Marian Saint and Doctor of the Church from the East who lived in the fourth century left, among his many writings, a brilliant *oratio*. In it he implores Our Lady to be always "present" to him as the One who assists and guides him, who presides over everything and *"takes him by the hand."*

St. Germanus of Constantinople (†733) clearly states that the Virgin Mary *"dwells among us"* and *"walks in our midst."* St. John Damascene (†749) speaks of Our Lady as *"indwelling within us,"* as She who has *"imprisoned my spirit."* St. Bernard of Clairvaux (†1153) writes that *"the entire universe shines through the presence of Mary."*

The witness of Saints and mystics in the second millennium of the Church is even more numerous still. We will recall only a few examples among many: St. Anthony of Padua (†1231) beseeches Our Lady to assist us *"with the protection of Thy presence."*

St. Francis de Sales (†1622) writes that, especially in places consecrated to Our Lady, he experiences *"by a certain unexpected and sudden sense, that I am in the presence of my Mother."*

St. Louis M. Grignion de Montfort (†1716) describes the intimate and ineffable experience in which Our Lady makes Herself *"interiorly present"* to him.

One time while standing in one of his houses St. John Bosco (†1888) said, *"Our Lady walks through this house and covers it with Her mantle."*

St. Therese of the Child Jesus (†1897) said that she lived *"entirely hidden under the veil of the Holy Virgin,"* that is to say, in the "presence" of Our Lady whose veil was a sensible sign.

It is therefore essential for us to live fully aware of this "presence" of the Immaculate, to live intimately by this "presence," to live continually immersed in this "presence" throughout the regular course of the day, whether at work or rest, whether filled with joy or sorrow. This "presence" must never be set aside nor forgotten! Listen to the loving concern with which St. Maximilian M. Kolbe wrote to his confreres: he recommended *"silence, frequent ejaculatory prayers, and a love ever more ardent towards the Immaculate which is nourished by accomplishing Her manifest will through Obedience, above all in the things which contrast with self-love and one's natural inclination; and then mutual understanding and a jovial serenity."*[89]

With a little reflection it is readily understood that, in reality, it is impossible to intensely live this "presence" of the Immaculate and not be assimilated and gradually transformed into Her. St. Maximilian, when recommending with insistence that the brothers linger and frequently speak with the Immaculate, explains that precisely in doing this one is steadily transformed into Her: *"Frequently pause and speak familiarly with Her."*[90] And even when one is engaged and very absorbed by his work, St. Maximilian writes that *"a brief ejaculatory prayer while one works is the best prayer, and it is very practical because it unites us constantly and always closer to the Immaculate as an instrument in the hand of our Mistress, and by this means we will attain the grace of the illumination of our intellect (in order to recognize Her will) and of the fortification of our will (in order to accomplish it)."*[91]

---

[89] SK 515
[90] SK 1367
[91] SK 373

CHAPTER 4
"PROXIMITY, POSSESSION, IDENTIFICATION"

There is a presence of Our Lady which can progressively become a presence of "proximity," a presence of "possession," and a presence of "identification" of the person with Her.

The fact is that Our Lady is present by grace to those consecrated to Her by the *Marian Vow*. This presence is already, from the outset, a presence of very close and loving *"proximity,"* at least on the part of Our Lady. If they correspond faithfully, this close and loving proximity will assimilate them slowly but surely into the Immaculate and effectively make them Her *"possession,"* that is to say, Her *"absolute property,"* in order thus to transform them, increasing within them a presence of *identification*.

In this way, they find themselves mystically enclosed and living within Her. She, for Her part, effectively lives entirely in them. Ven. Fr. Allegra explains this well when he writes, "Through these Marian mysteries to live in Mary is equivalent to the phrase: Mary lives in me; just as these biblical phrases are ambivalent: Christ lives in us and we live in Christ."[92]

> Here we have the *circularity* of "presence" in the *reciprocity* of "possession," which St. Louis de Montfort had already written about in his day. He states that when one gives himself entirely to Our Lady, being stripped of himself, She "gives Herself also entirely and in an ineffable manner to him who has given Her everything. She immerses him in Her graces; adorns him with Her merits; sustains him with Her power; enlightens him with Her light; inflames him with Her love; communicates to him Her virtues: Her humility, faith, purity." In this fashion it is brought about that "when this consecrated person belongs totally to Mary, Mary also belongs totally to this soul."[93]

> Shortly thereafter the Saint points out with fervor, "How happy is that man who has given himself to Mary, who has entrusted himself and lost himself completely in Mary! He is totally for Mary, and Mary is totally for him."[94] Further on he explains how Our Lady loves Her consecrated children

---
[92] *Il Cuore Immacolata di Maria, via a Dio*, p. 130.
[93] *True Devotion*, n. 144.
[94] Ibid., n. 179.

because "they are Her portion and inheritance,"[95] and he specifies that "She does not just love them with affection, but with efficacy. Her love for them is active and effective."[96]

Finally, in his text, *The Secret of Mary*, he writes that when there is the commitment to faithfully live one's consecration, "Mary comes to live in the soul in such wise that it is no longer the soul that lives, but it is Mary who lives in it and comes to be, so to speak, the soul of the very soul."[97] And here we have come to the mystical presence of *"identification."* Further on the Saint has the consecrated soul exclaim, "Mary is in me. Oh what a treasure! What a consolation! And will I not then be totally Hers from now on?"[98]

The presence of the Immaculate, therefore, becomes the presence of *possession* and *identification,* as St. Maximilian states. Consequently, it is really true that we can neither be, nor live, except in Her "presence." Through this "presence" She fully penetrates, invades, and possesses our most interior *"I,"* that is, our mind, our heart, our will, and our memory. *"She penetrates our soul,"* St. Maximilian says, *"and directs its faculties with an unlimited power. We truly belong to Her. Therefore, we are with Her, always and everywhere…"*[99]

This is the greatness of the *Marian Vow* faithfully lived out. It leads us ever higher, evermore towards *transubstantiation* into the Immaculate. It really and truly brings us to live *"with Her, always and everywhere."*

In this regard it is enough to recall again that expression of St. Pio of Pietrelcina who, in a letter to his Spiritual Father, was able to write, "My dear Mother… is always with me."[100] Another time, when he was all agitated and disturbed, he had a vision of the divine Mother with the Infant Jesus in Her arms; They said to him, *"Calm down! We are with you, you belong to Us and We to you."*[101] Another helpful episode is this: a confrere asked if Our Lady had ever appeared to him in his cell and Padre Pio immediately responded, *"Rather, ask me if Our Lady has ever left my cell!"*

---

95 Ibid., n. 201
96 Ibid., n. 202
97 *Il segreto di Maria*, n. 55.
98 Ibid., n. 66
99 SK 461
100 *Epistolario*, vol. I, p. 252.
101 *Epistolario*, vol. IV, p. 1024.

Likewise, on another occasion, St. Pio stated that Our Lady was always at his side on the altar during the celebration of Holy Mass. As a matter of fact, one of his spiritual children asked him if the Madonna was present at his Holy Mass and Padre Pio replied, *"Our Lady accompanies me to the altar every morning together with our Seraphic Father St. Francis, in order to celebrate the Mass."* Regarding the two years when he had to celebrate the Mass privately in the little Chapel of the friary, whenever someone asked him, "My Spiritual Father, in those years did you have to celebrate Mass by yourself?" Padre Pio would reply, *"I was never alone. Our Lady always kept me company during the Holy Mass."*

Among many episodes in the life of Ven. Fr. Gabriel, we read of one morning in particular, when, after his completion of the celebration of Holy Mass, one of his nieces asked him: "Uncle, why did you celebrate Holy Mass by yourself?" Fr. Gabriel answered in all simplicity, *"But I was not alone, Our Lady was there. Didn't you see Her?"*

"FIXED IDEA," "DRUG," "OBSESSION"

According to the thought of St. Maximilian, we speak of the *presence of possession* which the Immaculate has in each soul consecrated with the *Marian Vow*. In order to help us in reflecting on this, and to facilitate our understanding of it, we can make use of three very significant analogies which lend themselves well to illustrating this point and bring us to be able to better grasp the reality and importance of the Immaculate's *presence of possession* in the soul.

"Fixed idea"

The first analogy refers to that *fixed idea*, or that *madness of love*. We can compare this to that pathological state which, in medical circles, is called *paranoia*. This state brings with it a true and proper mental alteration or psychological disturbance which conditions the patient's entire thought and activity; he is completely ruled by this fixation.

So, if a person is to have the Immaculate in his mind as a *fixed idea*, or to have the Immaculate in his heart as one "mad in love" (as St. Maximilian once said of himself), then this means that in everything he is governed and led by the Immaculate, that She rules his mind and heart, and not for a passing moment or a brief space of time every now and then, but continuously. This *fixed idea* in the mind and constant "mad love" of the heart conditions all of his activity so that it may correspond to the demands and impulses of boundless love.

The "drug"

The second analogy is that of *drugs*. In our times, sad to say, we know all too well the devastating reality that drugs can have upon men and women, especially the youth. They are swept away by addiction to drugs, by this "plague" as it has rightly been defined: a "plague" which humiliates, enslaves, degrades, and even kills its victims in a frightful manner.

The drug addict, in fact, is literally ruled by *drugs* which penetrate, possess, and govern him, and lead him to do things that he certainly would never have done without them. He is ruled and completely dependent upon narcotics or alcohol which enslave him and clearly make him a *drug addict* or *alcoholic* who becomes unable to govern his own life according to right reason and common sense.

In the same way, he who has made the *Marian Vow* and lives in the presence of the Immaculate and assimilates himself to Her becomes, little by little, a *Marian addict*—one dependent upon Mary in thinking and acting always in a supernatural way, in rejoicing and suffering always with Her, in Her, and for Her.[102] It could be said that love for the Immaculate is for him that heavenly "drug" that possesses him, inspires him, directs him, and makes him act in a holy manner in every circumstance.

"Obsession"

The third analogy is that of diabolical *obsession*. This too is more frequent and lethal for mankind in these times when satanic sects and cults are multiplying. An *obsessed* person has a type of presence of the devil in himself; and usually it is a presence so active that the devil can even come to possess the person, substituting for the person in thought, work, and action. "We know about the obsessed,

---

[102] Cf. SK 508

those possessed by demons," writes St. Maximilian, *"by which the devil speaks, thinks and acts."*[103]

And so, analogously, the Immaculate wishes to make Herself present in the person consecrated to Her with the *Marian Vow*. She wants to "possess the person" by governing him with Her grace and according to Her good pleasure. St. Maximilian says, *"We want to be obsessed by Her and even more so, without limits, so that She Herself may think, speak, move by means of us."*[104] This is our desire, and in this way *"She alone"* will live in us, animating us with Her grace and making us Christ-like in every thought, word, and action. Then, and only then, shall the soul be able to truly say, paraphrasing the words of St. Paul, *"It is no longer I who live, but the Immaculate lives Jesus in me."*

"BUT ONE HEART IN HER"

In one of his beautiful letters to the friars, when St. Maximilian is describing his voyage on a ship, his close union with the Immaculate does not fail to shine forth in his words (he was, after all, continually in Her presence in his thought, concerns, and actions). This is what the Saint writes: *"…My dear, beloved children, surely you will guess what love the Immaculate, our dear Mother, showed me on Friday, the feast of Her seven Sorrows. To tell the truth, I suffered greatly. The waves were crashing against the ship, I was feeling weak, I remained laying down for a long time; it seemed to me that I was failing; I would have liked to get up and move myself, but then there came a cold sweat and the vomiting of seasickness […]. My headache did not decrease. During the night I was extremely tired […]. My only relief was the mental invocation which I made frequently, very frequently, of the Most Holy Name of Mary. Perhaps, in my delirium from the fever, I even forgot to do this at certain times.*

"Then I began to feel a little better; I opened my suitcase to see what they had put in it for us. I began to unpack it and… behold, the small head of a little statue of the Immaculate. How could I resist from kissing Her with tenderness? […]. Are we not but one heart in Her?"[105]

From this letter we can bring out two particular points about the "presence" of the Immaculate in the mind and heart of St. Maximilian during his agonizing voyage into the extreme Orient.

---
[103] SK 508
[104] Ibid.
[105] SK 503

Above all, we see the "presence" of the Immaculate in St. Maximilian's *mind* during a grave illness. His *"only relief was the mental invocation... made frequently, very frequently, of the Most Holy Name of Mary."* Note well that his invocation of the Name of Mary was *frequent, very frequent*; and, notwithstanding, he was worried that, *"Perhaps, in my delirium from the fever, I even forgot to do this at certain times."* Here we see the extreme delicacy of St. Maximilian's concern, namely, that *in his delirium from fever* he may have failed to invoke the Immaculate in his thoughts!... What can we say of ourselves, on the other hand?

Then we also clearly see the presence of the Immaculate in St. Maximilian's *heart*, especially when he opens the suitcase for his trip and, unpacking it, *"behold, the small head of a little statue of the Immaculate."* At that sight, his heart immediately leapt with joy; hence he writes, *"How could I resist from kissing Her with tenderness?"* In reality it was impossible for him to contain himself. Why? The answer is very simple, *"Are we not but one heart in Her?"*

What a splendid example this is of the reciprocal "presence" of love between the Immaculate and St. Maximilian. It is in this way that the *Marian Vow* must be constantly lived out: with affection, thought, intensity, and a union so intimate as to become without respite: *"but one heart in Her!"*

TAKE HEART AND DO NOT BE DISCOURAGED

Do we not perhaps have grounds to be saddened since we do not succeed in experiencing and living the sweet "presence" of the Immaculate, we who have the *Marian Vow*? Does it perhaps not depend entirely upon us, upon our generous efforts, our profound recollection, and our constant desire?

The experience of the mystical presence of the Immaculate, to be sure, is not bound up solely in the faithful efforts of an *ordinary* Marian devotion; rather, this experience demands and surely brings with it an *extraordinary* devotion and intimacy with the Immaculate which guides us along the way of *transubstantiation* into Her in order to more fully and perfectly *christify* us, even if we are unaware of what She is accomplishing in us with Her motherly action.

It may be possible to form an idea of this by recalling St. Pio's description of this experience to his spiritual father: *"I feel close and bound to the Son by means of this Mother, without even seeing the chains which so tightly hold me.*"[106] It was through the Mother, then, that St. Pio found himself bound to the Crucified Lord.

What can be said of St. Pio's union with his *"Bella Mammina"*—his "dear and beautiful little Mother?" He certainly lived in constant union with Her, an intense union of vibrant and burning love. With complete attention and no indolence whatsoever, he cultivated an extraordinary devotion to Her in which he was completely committed to maintaining Her sweet presence which was so intimately maternal. It is also well known that before he would even enter the confessional for hours on end, he would stop and pray each day for a couple of minutes before an image of the Immaculate, entrusting himself to Her so that She might be very, very close to him during the administration of the Sacrament of Penance; as a matter of fact, at the moment of sacramental absolution he always saw, *"Our Lady seated, in a way that only a mother could, on the judgment seat."*[107]

What can be said, on the other hand, about our union with the Immaculate? What a *deficit* of love we see in ourselves in Her regard! And so? Take heart and follow the examples of the great Marian Saints. So as not to become discouraged, let us recall here the comforting thought of St. Louis de Montfort who, in his hallowed book, *The Secret of Mary*, writes:

"Do not be afflicted and do not torment yourself with the fact that you cannot immediately rejoice in the sweet presence of the Virgin. This grace is not given to everyone and when God in His great mercy grants it, the soul, if it is not faithful in receiving it with great frequency, readily loses it. If a similar disgrace should happen to you, turn to Mary and mend your fault."[108]

---

[106] *Epistolario*, vol. I, p. 357.
[107] Cf. *Padre parla della Madonna*, p. 91.
[108] *The Secret of Mary*, n. 52

CHAPTER 5
THE MARIAN VOW AND THE THREE VOWS

In the form of religious life of the Franciscans of the Immaculate, the *Marian Vow* has a place of primary importance. It has a dynamic relationship with St. Francis of Assisi's *Regula Bullata* (the matrix of the entire form of the seraphic life) and with the three vows of religion (obedience, poverty, and chastity).

Its relationship with the other three vows of religion is a dynamic one on the level of grace with repercussions on the Franciscan life of virginity, poverty, and obedience. Through the *Marian Vow*, these three vows are assimilated into the consecrated life of the Immaculate Herself which is to be reproduced and prolonged within the Seraphic Order.

The *Marian Vow* is actually the first of the four vows. For this reason it bestows a specific spiritual configuration upon the other three vows, that is to say, it gives them a configuration that is fundamentally *Marian*. This recalls and renews for us the Franciscan origin of the Seraphic Order in that totally Marian "womb," the *Portiuncula* of St. Mary of the Angels in the plains of Assisi.

From this there immediately springs forth the meaningful and tender reference to the very origin of the Word Incarnate, namely the "womb" of the Immaculate Virgin. Her womb constitutes the Marian "root," the Marian "mode" of the redemptive Incarnation, as the Seraphic Doctor, St. Bonaventure teaches.

THE MARIAN-SERAPHIC "VOW"

It goes without saying that the *Marian Vow* characterizes and spiritually qualifies the very religious Profession of each Franciscan of the Immaculate. It is a religious vow which is constitutive and specific, and it has a spiritual value which is "totally absorbing." The religious Profession of the Franciscans of the Immaculate is permeated by the

Marian Vow in such wise that the three vows and the entire form of Franciscan life according to the *Seraphic Rule* and the Institute's Constitutions become marianized. It radically configures the form of life to that of the being and activity of the Immaculate, of She who is the person most supremely *Christ-conformed* and *christified*.

The *Marian Vow*, strictly binding on a par with the other three vows and in organic unity with them, expresses that which the classic triad of vows, common to the other Franciscan Orders, cannot express in and of themselves, namely, the *Marian-conformity*[109] of the Franciscan life. This *Marian-conformity* expressed by the *Marian Vow* is the evangelical matrix of the most perfect and complete *Christ-conformity* which we see shine forth in the principal patrons and models of the Franciscans of the Immaculate: the Seraphic Father, St. Clare, St. Maximilian and St. Pio of Pietrelcina.

Hence, the *Marian Vow*, with its most profound content, makes explicit the radical Marian dimension of the *Seraphic Order*. It constitutes the *proprium* [that is to say, what is particular and proper] of the charism and specific purpose of the Franciscan Friars and Sisters of the Immaculate in their life as "minors" or "lesser ones" according to the *Seraphic Rule*.

Along these lines it must also be added that the gift of the *Marian Vow* is the particular constitutive *raison d'être* of the Institute. Therefore it is placed at the foundation, and forms the specific justification of the freely made choice of the members of the Institute in responding to their call from God and sanctifying themselves accordingly by way of the Mary-formed life, which is the matrix of the Christ-formed life according to the *Seraphic Rule*.

One must also consider the fact that there is a sort of connatural relationship between the *Marian Vow* and the *Seraphic Rule*, like that found between the *Marian Vow* and the other three vows. This bond is one of abundant grace which unites them in profound synergy and assimilates them in full symbiosis within the very soul of the Seraphic Father. This was the intuition of St. Maximilian who, in this regard, intended to state in a precise manner the most intimate and vital Marian root of Franciscanism which shaped and animated the exalted evangelical character of his life which was so conformed to Christ.

---

109   *mariaformità* in Italian, translated as "conformity-to-Mary" or "Marian form" throughout this text.

Every Franciscan of the Immaculate by his religious Profession of the *Seraphic Rule,* and with the *Marian Traccia* and the *Constitutions* of the Institute, desires to live the evangelical life in its most perfect form. We are speaking here of the Franciscan form of life rooted in its womb of origin, which is the *Portiuncula* of St. Mary of the Angels, that is to say, rooted in the "womb" of its essential "Marian character," in order to reach the most exalted, seraphic christification within that "womb."

As a result of this, it can be said without hesitation that the *Marian Vow* introduces into the other three vows of religion and brings together within them a genuine Marian spirit. One could say that it marianizes the three vows, radicalizing their purest evangelical character for the maximum quotient of "conformity" to Jesus who was, in an entirely unique and primary way, *totally Marian,* just as He was totally obedient, totally poor, and totally chaste.

Far from being a vow which is to be placed alongside the other three vows of religion or simply an add-on to them, the *Marian Vow* is, by right and as a matter of fact, the *first* of the vows. This is because it is constitutive to that specific Marian-seraphic charism which penetrates, animates, and clothes the other three vows and the whole religious life of each Franciscan of the Immaculate.

According to St. Maximilian, the Immaculate should become the *"the soul of the Constitutions"* through unlimited consecration of the Seraphic Order to Her. It is for this reason that the *Marian Vow* sanctions the content and spirit with which the whole Franciscan life must be lived. It takes this life and thoroughly immerses it within the Immaculate, within Her Heart, and within Her womb. It is here that every friar and sister is formed and entirely reborn in Christ, as St. Maximilian so splendidly puts it: *"in the womb of the Immaculate the soul is reborn in the form of Jesus Christ."*[110]

This will all become evidently clear and concrete for us as we briefly reflect on the introspective analysis and give a rapid assessment of the intimate relationship which exists between the *Marian Vow* and each of the three vows of religion.

THE VOW OF OBEDIENCE

The vow of obedience receives a surge of special grace from the *Marian Vow* which brings the subject to see the Immaculate more

---
[110] SK 1295

readily in the person of the superior, specifically and in authority, in general. This disposes the friars and sisters to accept every order and command from Her, through "God's representative," regardless of how bitter or painful it may be (provided, of course, that what is asked is not sinful). This would also include the call to leave for distant and dangerous missionary lands, a command which the Franciscans of the Immaculate are ready to obey as docile instruments in the hands of the Immaculate.

Thus, the *Marian Vow* enlarges the ambit of obedience and goes beyond the limits established by the *Rule of St. Francis* (chapter XII). It makes the superior's authority radically unlimited, one could say, regarding what is licit. It radicalizes the submission and renouncement of the subject's self-will, feelings, and own way of seeing things by marianizing the obedience of the subject who is now held, by faith, to see the Immaculate in the superior and to obey the Immaculate through the superior. The subject is bound to obey just as the Immaculate obeyed God, as a humble *"handmaid of the Lord"* (Lk 1:38).

By virtue of the *Marian Vow*, therefore, the obedience of the friars and sisters becomes obedience *to* the Immaculate in constituted authority and becomes an assimilation with the obedience *of* the Immaculate to God in His "representative." If we reflect well on this reality of grace in the subject who must obey in virtue of the *Marian Vow*, we shall see that it is simultaneously sublime and terrifying: *sublime,* because it makes the subject obedient to the Immaculate and like the Immaculate; *terrifying,* because this is possible only by denying one's very self at the source, to the point of not even having a will of one's own, but having only the freedom of the Immaculate, and this can only come about as the fruit of a radical ascetical journey made completely in faith.

Hence, St. Maximilian was able to write that the essence of obedience is *"to belong to* Her *under every aspect. To annihilate oneself and become* Her. *The fundamental element of such a transformation consists in conforming, fusing, unifying our will with Hers."*[111]

The spirit of faith which must animate religious obedience is, therefore, essential and of primary importance in order to know how to see God's will in the orders of the superiors and to see the "representative of Christ" in the superiors (LG 37). St. Maximilian was very concerned about this fundamental aspect of religious

---

[111] SK 579

obedience and wrote, as a matter of fact, that *"I have become aware that certain religious allow themselves to be guided more by reason than by faith, more by the natural order than by the supernatural order; consequently they see their superiors as persons more or less wise and prudent rather than seeing them as representatives of God. Oh! Be very vigilant that this destructive plague, which deprives holy obedience of every merit, not attack the Brothers."*[112] And again, he explains and urges one of the brothers: *"With regard to our relationship with our superiors we cannot let ourselves be guided by natural motives, that is, by sympathy or antipathy, by one or the other or both of these feelings; but we must see in them, in a supernatural way, the will of the Immaculate, and as such accomplish Her will with joy."*[113]

> Who, in fact, can measure St. Maximilian's vision of faith in obedience when he found himself in the concentration camp of Auschwitz? He never rebelled when exercising obedience to those criminal superiors and tolerating their tyrannical wickedness; rather, he prayed and suffered for them. It was the trial by fire for his supernatural vision of faith which always saw and accepted the will and permissions of God, and which imitated the divine example of Jesus who became *"obedient to death, even to death on a cross"* (Ph. 2:8), that is to say, obedient to the most unjust and ignominious death.

> We recall that when St. Maximilian was treated in a beastly fashion by the *Gestapo* guards of Auschwitz, he did not rail against them nor react in any way except in offering all to the Immaculate, being patient and tolerant. He would explain and tell his companions of misfortune: *"It is all for our dear Mother!"*

> And what of St. Pio of Pietrelcina? When his faculties for Confession were taken away and the possibility of celebrating Holy Mass in public was removed, he listened to the decree of his condemnation in silence and, after it was read, said, *"Fiat voluntas Dei"* ("Thy will be done"), and headed immediately to the choir to pray. And so for more than two years he, perhaps the greatest Confessor the

---
[112] SK 128
[113] SK 609; cf. also SK 660

Church has ever known, was deprived of his faculties to hear Confessions. It is always true that the pure obedience of faith is realized, above all, in heroic denial of self.

THE VOW OF POVERTY

The *Marian Vow* enriches the vow of Franciscan poverty which is already, in itself, quite radical. Indeed, it demands an even more radical "expropriation" of self through the concrete privation of everything, through a total, interior detachment from things, persons, places, and work.

The entire being of each Franciscan who professes the *Marian Vow* becomes the "absolute property" of the Immaculate. Therefore, they all belong to Her even to the point of losing themselves entirely in Her, of becoming not only Her servant, Her slave, but even Her "instrument," an "object" in Her immaculate hands, of being utterly reduced to "nothing" for Her and in Her.

In order to realize the most perfect form of Franciscan-Marian life, we—as it is written in the *Traccia Mariana* ("The Marian Plan of Franciscan Life")—"*want to be 'instruments,' 'things,' 'nothing' in the hands of the Immaculate Mediatrix, our Mother Coredemptrix and Queen,* unconditionally, unlimitedly, irrevocably *consecrated to Her, even to the point of identifying ourselves with Jesus in the most perfect way possible…* A word from St. Maximilian: '*Our life must be a prolongation of Jesus on this earth by means of Mary*' (Conf. of July 15, 1936), by imitating the Immaculate '*in the same way as She imitated Jesus,*' imitating St. Francis '*as he imitated Jesus.*'[114]"

The desire to be "nothing" is a sort of true "annihilation" for Her and in Her. This desire hopes to arrive at the state of the *"kenosis"* (self-emptying) of the Word made flesh who became a *"slave"* for our sakes (Phil 2:7). It hopes to imitate the *kenosis* of the humanity of Christ which was deprived even of a human personality of its own. In this being "nothing" there is accomplished that word of the Holy Spirit written by the Apostle: God has chosen "the things that are not" (*ea quae non sunt*: 1 Cor 1:28) in order "to bring to naught the things that are" (*ut confunderet ea quae sunt*).

There is one particular detail which helps us to understand and appreciate the specific radicalization of vowed poverty demanded by

---

[114] SK 339

the *Marian Vow* with respect to the simple religious vow of poverty. That particular is this: the Franciscan who has made the *Marian Vow* expropriates himself even of all personal merits and spiritual goods (the fruit of his prayers and sacrifices).

Yes, as St. Louis M. Grignion de Montfort explicitly points out, "no vow of poverty, even in the most austere religious Order, demands an expropriation like this."[115] This radical expropriation, then, is truly an added grace—grace upon grace.

Hence, the Franciscan who has made the *Marian Vow* and is fully faithful in putting it into practice can repeat all the more with St. Francis of Assisi: *"My God and my all!"* and with St. Maximilian M. Kolbe: *"My Immaculate and my all!"*

THE VOW OF CHASTITY

The *Marian Vow* embellishes the vow of chastity. It marianizes the entire person, body and soul, through the various phases of active and passive purification, all of which work together for one's transfiguration or transubstantiation into the Immaculate, into Her who is that transparent and radiant icon of the Word Incarnate.

The Immaculate is the Ever-Virgin, the Virgin most pure, the Virgin of virgins, the Queen of the Angels, and Queen of virgins. If, then, the operation of "absorption" into the Immaculate is connatural with the *Marian Vow*, it is obvious that by such "absorption," the chastity of the friars and sisters is, in a certain sense, absorbed in Her so as to transfigure them via the most intact and candid virginity of the Immaculate.

Thus, the virginal purity of the Immaculate, with all the nuances of divine beauty which adorn it, will shine forth brightly in the friars and sisters who faithfully live the *Marian Vow* and will envelop them with the fragrance of lilies. Through the *Marian Vow*, therefore, consecrated chastity becomes an even greater reminder to everyone of the *"things that are above"* (Col 3:2), a support in refusing all the *"dung"* of this world, as St. Paul puts it (Phil 3:8), a strength and persevering grace in avoiding all that which is not God and does not lead to God.

In the measure in which they give themselves unlimitedly to the Immaculate, to Her who is *"the brightness of eternal light,"* She will give the most intimate grace of participating in Her lily-like

---

115 *The Secret of Mary*, n. 29.

purity and radiance which will make them holy *"in body and in spirit"* (I Cor 7:34).

In this way, the practice of an entirely immaculate Franciscan life is made easier. It is rooted in the most profound, total, pure, and exclusive love of God; it is enriched by the gifts of motherly tenderness, spousal delicacy, and virginal fragrance. All of these are proper to the Immaculate and transfigure chastity into holy immaculateness which is fragrant and wholly radiant of divine love.

The *Marian Vow*, therefore, marianizes the consecrated chastity of Franciscans of the Immaculate. It carries the vow of chastity to the most exalted immaculateness of divine love in mind and heart, in the interior and exterior senses, in the attitude and behavior of "an angelic life of sweet-smelling fragrance," as Bl. Thomas of Celano wrote in speaking of the first community of friars who lived at St. Mary of the Angels.[116] All of this also shines forth in a particular way in the person of St. Clare of Assisi who is rightly portrayed with a lily in her hand, that bright symbol of the virginal life of the Immaculate. So, too, in St. Gertrude who was specifically defined as the *"resplendent Lily of the Most Holy Trinity."*

This accounts for St. Maximilian's severity regarding the custody of this precious, yet fragile virtue. He even imposed upon the friars "by virtue of holy obedience and under the pain of grave sin" to refer to him *"any word, act or transgression which, at Niepokalanòw, might undermine the virtue of chastity."*[117]

THE "PROPRIUM" OF THE MARIAN VOW

At this point we do well to ask what specifically and profoundly differentiates the *Marian Vow* from the other three vows of religion that delineate the life consecrated to God. In other words, what is the *proprium* of the *Marian Vow*; what is its specific character?

Everyone is aware that in religious life the vow of obedience requires the renouncement of one's own free will in order to possess and live in the freedom of the infinite will of God. The vow of poverty requires the renouncement of possessing anything as "one's own" in order to possess the infinite riches of God (the *Deus meus et omnia*—"*my God and my All*" of St. Francis of Assisi). The vow of chastity requires the renouncement of the human, spousal love of

---

[116] Cf. Celano, *Second Life of St. Francis*, 19 (FF 605).
[117] Cf. G. Lentini, *Massimiliano Kolbe*, p. 285.

marriage in order to have the divine, spousal love of the infinite God, the "Bridegroom of the soul."

So then, what renouncement is required by the *Marian Vow* in terms of its relationship with God? With some reflection, we see that the *Marian Vow* demands the total renunciation of the entire human person—the "I," the *ego*—with all of its potential (the person here is reduced to a "thing," a "nothing"), so as to possess the potential of the person—the "I," the *ego*—of the Immaculate (through transubstantiation in Her). That renunciation is only partial in the three vows apart from the Marian. So the *Marian Vow* gives to the soul, a *Bride of God* (by virtue of the religious Profession), a likeness or assimilation to the soul of the Immaculate whose soul is wholly *virginal-spousal* and wholly *virginal-maternal*. This is why Mary, the Bride of the Holy Spirit and wholly transubstantiated into the Holy Spirit,[118] became Mother of God by the power of the Holy Spirit.[119]

As we know, the infinite wellspring of every instance of divine fruitfulness has its *proprium* in the *Father's* fontal plenitude of goodness.[120] It could be said that with the Incarnation, the *humanization* of the paternal fruitfulness and love of God has been realized in the *New Eve*, who is Mary. St. Maximilian speaks clearly of this in one of his conferences: *"Jesus is the Son of God and Son of Mary. The heavenly Father and Mary have the same Son, Jesus, the same object of generation, [which is] eternal from the Father, temporal from the Mother [...]. On earth Mary participates in the paternal love of God regarding Jesus; [She] dilated, prolonged, and continued the Father's love on earth by adjoining it to Her Mother's love, with exceptional, maternal sentiments of blood and affection. At Jesus' baptism and transfiguration the Father proclaims: 'This is My beloved Son,' presenting Him to the world; and Mary too can say: Jesus is the entire object of my love and care, at Bethlehem, in Egypt, at Nazareth, everywhere and always."*[121]

With the consecration made in the *Marian Vow* we radically renounce the possession of ourselves so as to be the *"absolute property"* of the Immaculate. Consequently, our souls are transfigured into the Immaculate and become partakers of the being and acting of the Immaculate as divine Mother and universal Mediatrix of all graces.

---

[118] Cf. CK [= *Ascetical Conferences* of St. Maximilian in Polish.] 26 Nov., 1938.
[119] Cf. SK 1318
[120] Cf. St. Bonaventure, *Breviloquium*, p. 1, ch 1 and 2.
[121] V. Di Lillo, *Incontri con Padre Massimiliano*, pp. 33–34 [English version: *Roman Conferences of St. Maximilian*, pp. 23–24].

The *Marian Vow*, therefore, *marianizes* us and leads us decisively to *"disappear"*[122] and *"be annihilated"*[123] in the Immaculate, conforming us to the divine Mother and Mediatrix who brings forth God and all graces. In other words, we could say that its Marian character[124] comes to impress upon the soul the Maternity of Mary whose origin is the fontal plenitude of the Father. For Mary's motherhood, rooted in the fecundity of the Father, can be said to present itself as the *"created"* mold of that divine fontal plenitude of goodness.

At this point we are able to appreciate the divine reality of the mystery of the *begetting of Christ* which is proper to the Immaculate Virgin Mother of God. Graced with the *Marian Vow*, we come to participate in this reality and, as a result, *"the more a soul becomes similar to the Immaculate,"* writes St. Maximilian, *"all the more does it become the mother of Jesus in a supernatural way in his own heart."*[125] Besides this, the Saint specifies that Blessed Mary *"is the Immaculate Conception. Consequently, She is such also in us and She transforms us into Herself as immaculate ones... She is the Mother of God; and She is the Mother of God also in us... and She makes us gods and mothers of God who generate Jesus Christ in the souls of men... What sublimity!..."*[126]

It is evident, then, that the *Marian Vow* of total consecration to the Immaculate entails more than a merely private consecration. Those with the Vow are called, according to the thought of St. Maximilian, to "be marianized" as *"the mothers of God who beget Jesus Christ in the souls of men."* Mary's divine Maternity—which has its origin in the divine Paternity of God—makes the soul capable of bringing forth Jesus in order to give Him to souls.

> What is more, St. Maximilian also writes and explains the dimension of our assimilation with the Immaculate so as to give birth to Her in souls: *"We are Hers, of the Immaculate, unlimitedly Hers, perfectly Hers; we are, as it were,* Her very self [...] *She is of God to the point of becoming His Mother, and we want to become the mother which gives birth to the Immaculate in all hearts that exist and that shall be [...]. May She, in entering*

---

[122] SK 508
[123] SK 579
[124] *marianità* in Italian, translated as "Marian character, dimension, or quality" throughout this text.
[125] SK 1273
[126] SK 486

these hearts and taking possession of them in the most perfect way, give birth there to the sweet Jesus, to God…"[127]

Therefore, it is also clear that the *Marian Vow* lived out fully is capable of bringing about the marianization of the soul by giving it a fecundity capable of bringing forth *"the Immaculate in all hearts"* so that She, the Immaculate, might enter the hearts of men in order to *"give birth there to the sweet Jesus, to God…"*

THE "MATRIX" OF TRINITARIAN EXEMPLARISM

The Marian character, fecundity and maternity[128] of the *Marian Vow* are three realities of inestimable value which come from the mystery of the Virgin Mary. These three are found together in our souls and work to assimilate us completely to the Mother of the Word Incarnate, the "created" motherly mold of the "uncreated" fontal plenitude of goodness in the Father.

Indeed, the divine Word and Son of God originates by eternal generation from the Father. Whereas the *Begetting of Christ* in time originates with the "created" divine Maternity of a mere creature, in the person of Mary, by the working of the Holy Spirit; that is to say, Mary conceived and brought forth the Word Incarnate, the God-Man, the Son of the Most High who became Her Son, *"the Son of man."* So through the *Marian Vow,* Mary's divine Maternity penetrates our souls and *maternalizes* them. She confers on them that *Marian form* whereby our souls attain that very conformity-to-Christ realized in the Immaculate Herself. They are made in some way partakers of her fecundity to *Beget Christ*, the very fecundity by which She conceived and gave birth to Jesus Christ, the God-Man.

We may say, therefore, that the *Marian Vow*, lived in the fullness of this marianization, sets the soul on its journey towards the Most Holy Trinity. This is the very journey by which the Immaculate was ineffably inserted into the very inner life of the Trinity, precisely because She belonged to the order of the hypostatic union as the Mother of the Incarnate Word by the working of the Holy Spirit. Hence, She is called with the Holy Spirit the *complementum*

---
[127] SK 508
[128] *marianità, fecondità,* and *maternità* in Italian.

sanctissimae Trinitatis, i.e., the complement or fulfillment of the mutual love of Father and Son.[129]

To complete the profound *Trinitarian* connotation which penetrates the mystery, mission, and person of Blessed Mary, it is not difficult, by way of analogy and with the proper distinctions being made, to grasp as a kind of golden thread that unity which exists between:

- the Father and Mary as his first born daughter chosen by him to be Mother of his Only-begotten and beloved Son;

- the divine Son of God and the Father's first born daughter whom the Son desired to be His Mother and whom He preserved from all taint of original sin (who for this reason is defined by the great poet Dante Alighieri as, precisely, *"the Daughter of your Son"*[130]);

- the Holy Spirit, the "uncreated" Immaculate Conception, who "transubstantiates" the very being of the first-born daughter of the Father and Mother of His Son to become the icon of the Holy Spirit and Complement of Father and Son, the "created" Immaculate Conception of Mary Most Holy (in a certain sense, there is here a divine, *spousal* unity between them), according to the teaching of St. Maximilian.[131]

At this point reflection should be given to the masterly teaching of St. Bonaventure about *Trinitarian exemplarism*, based on the *exitus* of all things from the Father and their *reditus* to him through Christ and Mary (cf. Jn 16: 28), an *exitus-reditus* also reflecting the Marian antiphon of the *Office of the Passion* composed by St. Francis.[132] It finds its highest and supreme realization—or better still, its sublime *matrix*—here, at the summit and in the fullness of the mystery of Mary Immaculate. She is presented as the unrivalled *paradigm* of the mystery of the inner life of the

---

[129] Cf. SK 634; 1318
[130] *Paradiso*, XXXIII, 1.
[131] Cf. SK 1318
[132] Cf. J. Schneider, *Virgo Ecclesia facta*.

Blessed Trinity and as its unique and most perfect "icon," by being:

- *the transparency* of the Father, as *Daughter*,

- *the transparency* of the Son, as *Mother*,

- *the transparency* of the Holy Spirit, as *Bride*.

St. Maximilian cites the Marian Antiphon of St. Francis in the same Roman conference cited just above[133] and enables us to know and love the Mother of God more profoundly in the mystery of Christ and of the Church. We see precisely in this Antiphon the wonder and mystery of the divine Maternity contemplated by St. Maximilian.[134] Mary is Mother in relation to the Son, not the Father of whom she is the first born daughter, the most perfect of created persons, most perfect because the created Immaculate Conception, fruit of the love of Father and Incarnate Son in the economy of salvation and so the "vertex" of love, the point where all the love of the Blessed Trinity whose complement is the Holy Spirit, meets all the love of creation (including that of the Angels) in Mary Immaculate. At this point the action of the Creator whose origin is the fontal plenitude of the Father reaches its term and finds in the love of the Immaculate Virgin a reaction equal and contrary to the love of Father and Son, and so begins the return of all creatures to the Father: through and in Mary to Christ and through and in Christ to the Father.[135]

Who is the divine Mother, asks St. Maximilian? A mere creature, but not simply another creature. She is the first born, beloved daughter of the Father, the created Immaculate Conception, basis of the power to conceive the Son of God and initiate the return of all things to the Father. We note: the order of processions in the Trinity and in the work of creation is from Father through Son to Holy Spirit-Mary. That order is neatly reversed in the return to the Father

---

[133] Di Lillo, *Incontri*, p. 33; also in SK 1286.
[134] Cf. SK 1320
[135] Cf. SK 1318; on action-reaction cf. SK 1286; 1291.

or reaction of creation in Mary to the love originating in the Father: from Mary, because spouse of the Holy Spirit, therefore Mother of God, and through Christ her Son to the Father.[136]

And we can say that St. Maximilian synthesizes all of this with clarity and essential conciseness when he writes, *"In a supernatural way the Mother of Jesus comes forth from the Father, the Son, and the Holy Spirit."*[137] She is presented as the radiant "icon" of the mystery of the Most Holy Trinity; therefore, *"where She enters, She brings with Herself the Most Holy Trinity."*[138] And *"in the union of the Holy Spirit with Her not only does love conjoin two Beings, but the first of them is all the love of the Most Holy Trinity, while the second is all the love of creation, and thus in such a union heaven is united with earth, the entire heavens with the entire earth, all Uncreated Love with all created love: This is the vertex of love."*[139]

---

[136] Cf. SK 1291; 1318
[137] SK 1273
[138] SK 991, paragraph O
[139] SK 1318

CHAPTER 6
THE MARIAN VOW AND THE FRATERNAL LIFE

Religious life in general and our religious life in particular, can well be said to be a life in the "Cenacle" or "Upper Room." It is the life of a family, of a fraternity which daily gathers around the domestic table, around the Eucharistic Table, and around Mary, the sweet Mother of Jesus and Mother of our religious family of the *Franciscans of the Immaculate*.

The *Marian Vow* is a stimulus for the community to live out the maternal "presence" of Mary which is living, constant, holy, and loving. How could it be otherwise? Our Lady is the "Mother" of our religious community and everyone knows that in a family the reality most "present" and operative is that of motherhood. It is the mother's presence which makes the family so close-knit and vital. The mother's presence is truly the most valuable and delightful treasure of every family. The "mother" is the soul of family unity; she is the family's administrator and guide by a grace proper to her, a grace which is connatural with motherhood itself according to God's creative design.

It is no surprise, then, that St. Maximilian, in order to guarantee the best possible "fraternal life" and provide for its increase, primarily recommended love for the Immaculate and union with Her. *"The more each one of us draws near to the Immaculate, the more we will draw near to one another: this unity is our strength!"*[140]

> The meaningful *oratio* of St. Ephrem is most enlightening and efficacious for grasping the maternal function of the *Marian Vow* for both the fraternal life of the entire religious community and for the spiritual life of each single member. In his *oratio* the Saint begs Our Lady to be always *present* in his actions and conversations, in his thoughts and desires, in

[140] SK 571

his entire way of behaving, in his every movement of soul and body; and he specifically asks Her to be present as *assistens, dirigens, praesidens, manuducens,* [that is to say, a presence which assists, directs, governs and leads by the hand].

Based on these words of St. Ephrem it is not difficult to comprehend how the *Marian Vow* by its very nature carries within itself this personal and constant presence of the Immaculate precisely as Mother. She is present as She who:

- *assists* continuously the religious community as a whole and each member individually;

- *directs* everything in every detail both for the religious community and for each of the religious who is consecrated to Her;

- *governs* the entire being and activity of the community and each single member;

- *leads by the hand* the community as a whole and its individual members.

If we are, therefore, all being *"led by the hand"* of the Immaculate, should this not encourage us to live the *Marian Vow* intensely by living in Her loving, motherly "presence" in its essence and simplicity?

MARIANIZE" THE FRATERNAL LIFE

If all of the members of the Franciscans of the Immaculate have pronounced the *Marian Vow*, they not only form a unity in their love for the Immaculate as their common Mother, but by virtue of such a Vow each one must strive to reach the point of *"being the Immaculate to one another."* When this happens, it is a sure sign that the marianization of the environment and fraternal life within the religious house are running on it on their natural track. This makes concrete that most fruitful form of fidelity to our seraphic-Marian vocation by the practice of the heroic virtues in conformity with the *Book of Sanctification*.

St. Maximilian M. Kolbe, as also St. Louis M. Grignion de Montfort, wished that all those who were consecrated to the Immaculate might arrive at *"breathing Mary."* [141] So "breathing Mary" must become the characteristic note of faithfully living the *Marian Vow*. It must be the natural atmosphere which animates every religious house of the Franciscans and Poor Clares of the Immaculate (every *Casa Mariana, Casa dell'Immacolata, Roseto*).

The living presence of the Immaculate in each Marian religious house must, by virtue of the *Marian Vow*, invade and occupy every time and place. This should be evident even by means of the simplest signs—i.e., images of the Immaculate in the cells and along the corridors, a little statue of the Immaculate where we are working, etc.—and by means of simple and humble reminders, such as the mutual greeting *"Ave Maria!"* upon seeing one another, the chiming of the Ave Maria melody of Lourdes or Fatima at each hour, etc.

One should be able to say of every Marian friary and convent of the Franciscans of the Immaculate that the Immaculate is truly and constantly present. Why? Because She lives there, walking its environs, entering the individual cells, and remaining among the sons and daughters consecrated to Her.

Thus, by virtue of living faithfully the *Marian Vow*, every Marian friary and convent (including each contemplative house—*Colombaio, Ritiro Mariano,* and *Roseto*) cannot help but become:

> - A prolongation of Nazareth, where Jesus lived thirty years of His life ever in the presence of Our Lady in that ineffable mystery of a loving union with Her, always speaking familiarly with Her, depending on Her and St. Joseph as a most amiable Son;
>
> - A continuation of the *Portiuncula* of St. Mary of the Angels, where St. Francis and St. Clare found their entirely Marian place of birth and became living images of the Crucified (St. Francis) and of the divine Mother (St. Clare);
>
> - A multiplication of the *Niepokalanów* in the time of St. Maximilian. In those barracks and among those friars who

---

[141] Cf. SK 614, 634

were Her "absolute property" it is not difficult to imagine that the Immaculate, full of motherly solicitude, really walked in their midst.

Fixing our gaze upon these models of origin for every Marian friary and convent, we cannot help but reflect upon that special "presence" of the Immaculate. She is present as the Mother and Queen of the whole community as well as of each friar and sister who has become "Her property" and lives in total dedication and unlimited service to Her for the benefit of themselves and souls to be saved.

We are speaking, therefore, of living the *Marian Vow* in a *coherently*, not in *mediocrity*. The *Marian Vow* must be lived in perfect observance of the *Book of Sanctification* so that it may bestow grace to the entire religious community by assimilating it to the *Holy Family* at Nazareth, the *Portiuncula*, and *Niepokalanòw*. St. Maximilian writes in this fashion: *"I must do everything in order to belong ever more and more to the Immaculate […] in order to become similar to Her, living by Her, so that my living environment might be illuminated more and more brightly by Her."*[142] Why? Because it is certain that *"a soul that loves the Immaculate truly from the heart, no matter where he finds himself, will instill his own love for the Immaculate into the environment which surrounds him."*[143]

In the *Process of Beatification, section on virtues*, of St. Maximilian we read testimonies from his fellow friars who stated that when the Saint was in the community and "he spoke to us with the utmost sentiment about Our Lady, there emanated from him a superior force" and "he conquered us all" because "we had the impression when he was speaking that he was not a man of this world."[144]

If a Marian friary or convent distances itself from fidelity to these models of origin (Nazareth, *Portiuncula*, and *Niepokalanòw*), then it would lose the fountainhead of its authenticity and specific charism. As a result, that community would signal and set into motion its own decline first along the path of "mitigations," then heading towards the path of an outright "decadence" of infidelity. Hence, that community would inevitably become incapable of producing fruit. It would render sterile the grand gift bestowed to it by God in the *Marian Vow* which is a gift laden with the potential

---

[142] SK 1251
[143] SK 892
[144] Cf. SK 456, 457, 573, 395–6, 636, 638

grace of elevation and growth in holiness (the *easiest and most sublime* holiness possible) and for the salvation of souls (the most *extensive* possible, extending even to the ends of the earth).

In every community (whether it be a small Marian house or a large Marian city), in all times and places, therefore, may there never be lacking that constant attention to keep intact the primacy of prayer and daily mortification harmonized with *vita perfecte communis* (the perfect common life) according to what has been laid down in the *Book of Sanctification*.

May each member of each community be ever animated in all things by that utterly supernatural triptych of grace which, in substance, carved out the life and person of St. Maximilian. Each of the Franciscans of the Immaculate must be carved out by the same means, namely:

- The *fixed idea*, which is the Immaculate;

- The *mad love* for the Immaculate;

- The *feverish action* for the Immaculate.

The Eucharist is that *"Bread made by the Mother,"* that is by the Immaculate, and is the *"Bread of the strong"* which sustained the Apostles, Confessors, Martyrs, and Virgins even in the most terrible and bloody of persecutions. This being the case, may every Marian friary and convent, and even more so those of the contemplative communities (every *Colombaio, Ritiro Mariano,* and *Roseto* of the Immaculate) seek to faithfully cultivate not only the daily Marian prayer of Rosaries prayed in common and in private, but also, and even more so, continuous Eucharistic Adoration where it is possible, at least during the daytime. In this way, the entire community will be able to continually find itself again and again united with the Immaculate around Him who must be the King and center of the love of our consecrated hearts. After all, He is that vital wellspring of grace that sanctifies and saves the whole universe.

BEWARE OF THE 'ITCH FOR NOVELTY' (CF. 2 TM 4:3)

The atmosphere of each Marian house, as well as the lifestyle of each of its members who are animated and characterized by the *Marian Vow*, must be protected and defended from that poisonous *"itch"* for novelty of which the Apostle Paul speaks (2 Tm 4:3). We are referring to that "itch" which continually tends to influence and seduce even the "elect," that is consecrated souls. And this is readily found in our day and age. Such novelty is presented in a wide-open and high impact fashion so as to gain hearing and welcome even into religious communities. Following this path always brings disaster to religious discipline and produces confusion of thought which together result in the dissolution of the ascetical life and, consequently, of the life of grace.

Following the school of St. Maximilian, we know well that the *Marian Vow* by its very "unlimited nature" excludes nothing which is good and licit in any field that might increase the universal and saving mission of the Immaculate Mediatrix. Rather, the *Marian Vow* leads to an openness to everything and seeks to utilize all that is "new"; however, always and exclusively in order to marianize it. Attention must be given to avoid being subjugated to the "new," and thus watering down or, worse still, deforming our way of life through compromising the very life *perfecte communis* (perfect common life) according to the *Book of Sanctification* which is our perennial form of life, totally rooted theologically, totally seraphic, totally Franciscan, and totally Marian.

Continual "vigilance" therefore demands that we humbly and insistently rely on "prayer" in accord with the teaching of Jesus, *"Watch and pray, that you may not enter into temptation"* (Mt 26:41). What temptation? The temptation, for example, to diminish the community times for prayer (5 hours daily), to mitigate the sharpness or reduce the communal and personal sacrifices of the penitential life (observance of silence and the cloister, fasts, enduring the winter cold, taking the discipline and religious discipline in general, modesty and reserve in dealing with the laity, etc.).

Beware of the "false plain!" This is the deadly path of the *"serpent,"* who slowly brings the soul to slither and slip down upon seemingly flat ground. In this way, he succeeds in carrying the soul to destruction, step by step, in a way that goes undetected and is almost impossible to recognize... May the Immaculate save us from this!

If anything, let us always keep in mind that now and in the future one should rather seek only to increase the times of community and personal prayer, the austerities of penance, and the privations of poverty, always, of course, with due discretion and maintaining the serenity of the fraternal life.

Certainly, the primary and most precious possession of the Franciscan fraternal life is the solid and faithful seraphic life lived with personal and communal commitment and entirely marked by the living "presence" of the Immaculate, our Mother and Queen. This is the primary goal of each religious and of each community to be realized through living out the *Marian Vow* with generosity; it is furthermore the primary gift to the community. All of this must come about under the direction of obedience to the superior which guarantees that everything be in accord with the will of the Immaculate. St. Maximilian explains this well noting that when our every project or idea has the seal of obedience, *"only then can we be certain that such is the will of the Immaculate, whereas I have much fear of occasionally adding something from my 'fetid garden.'"*[145]

It must always be kept in mind that the religious community becomes a most authentic and concrete image of our Holy Mother the Church only when the *Marian Vow* is lived out faithfully in the fraternal life through a regular observance of the *vita communis* (common life). Without this, the community will not reflect the image of the Church and, thus, will not become the truest and most real image of the *"Virgin made Church"* as St. Francis of Assisi so splendidly called Our Lady.[146]

THE "PRESENCE" OF THE MOTHER AND MEDIATRIX

St. Maximilian links the active "presence" of the Immaculate in a particular way with Her mission as Mother and Mediatrix. We do well, in fact, to cull St. Maximilian's teaching on the "presence" of the Immaculate from his life and writings:

- a personal, real, and active presence, as Her motherhood in action is personal and real,

- an active presence which brings forth grace, as Her universal mediation is fruitful in bearing grace.

It can be said beyond doubt that the personal "presence" of the Immaculate to each of the redeemed, as well as the whole of mankind,

---
[145] SK 347
[146] *Salutation of the Blessed Virgin* (FF 259).

reaches as far as Her motherhood and mediation extend. It cannot be otherwise. Wherever Mary's motherhood and mediation arrive, there too must be the personal and real presence of the Mother and Mediatrix, in soul and body, even if in an invisible manner. Being always precedes acting (*Operatio sequitur esse*).

A true and proper motherhood and mediation "at a distance" (*in distans*) is unthinkable. As we know, upon the earth the Immaculate was always near and present to Her Son Jesus, and even in Heaven Her place is always at His side. This is the divine plan: the Mother and the Son are always united and close to one another. If this is the plan regarding the Mother with Her *"Firstborn Son,"* that plan cannot be different regarding the Mother with Her second-born, third-born, and so on, right up until the last child who will live upon the face of the earth at the end of salvation history.

If it is not possible for earthly mothers to remain ever near their own children when far away, and if they then have to seek to be near their offspring merely by thought and affection at a distance (*in distans*), this is not the case with Our Lady. By virtue of the *transcendence* of Her divine, spiritual motherhood and Her universal maternal mediation which is in action always and everywhere, our divine Mother and Mediatrix has been granted this possibility to remain near Her children always. As is known, *transcendence* is not subject to the earthly laws of time and space.

If, then, Mary is Mother and universal Mediatrix, it is certainly not merely in the sense of an ideal or abstraction which is distant and generic in regard to all Her children and to each in particular. If the mother is always the person who is most proximate and concrete to each child, if she is the most real and personal to him, and if she is the one most intimately bound to her child in a personal relationship which is indestructible, then this applies in an *eminent* manner regarding the union between the divine Mother and each of the children to whom She has given birth *"in the order of grace,"* as Vatican II explains (LG 61).

What is more, if the "presence" of mother and child is the most personal, real, close, and vital that two human persons can have and whose love arrives at the most complete mutual assimilation, then such cannot but apply all the more in the relationship of that "co-presence" between the divine Mother and each of Her children.

Biologically speaking, it is known that for a certain amount of time newborn babes feel and recognize themselves to be "entirely one" with their mother, a true "part" of her. This is because the newborn babe takes his very life from her, is nourished by her, and grows bound to her vital presence.

If all of this applies to the relationship of love and union between every earthly mother and her child on the natural and corporal level, how much more does this apply on the supernatural and spiritual level! With what incomparable heights and depths does not all of this apply to the relationship of love and union between the divine Mother-Mediatrix and each of the children She has borne "in the order of grace?"

Has not St. Maximilian expressly written that with unlimited consecration to the Immaculate—and even more so with the *Marian Vow* of unlimited consecration—we come to be assimilated to the Immaculate so as even to become a *"part"* of the Immaculate? In fact here is how he so clearly and decisively writes: *"But what must we think of ourselves? Let us disappear in Her! May She alone remain, and we in Her, a part of Her."*[147] This is exactly what we become with the *Marian Vow*: *"a part of Her!"*

UNITING AND IDENTIFYING ONESELF WITH THE IMMACULATE "MOTHER"

The most precious, yet fragile goal of the "fraternal life" of the Franciscans of the Immaculate is none other than the complete *personal assimilation* of each friar or sister to the Immaculate in Her mission and reality as *"Mother."* In other words, we are speaking of an assimilation to Her in an affective manner, above all by making our own the dimension of Mary that is affective and *maternal*.

The simple yet essential expression, *"May you each be the Immaculate one to another,"* indicates first and foremost that we are replete and re-clothed with Her *maternal*, affective character. This cannot help but be "proper" to the *Marian Vow* since it is supposed to transubstantiate us into the Immaculate.

The "motherhood" of St. Francis

Is not this precisely what our Seraphic Father St. Francis taught us by his example and teaching? This affective dimension in a *maternal* key is exactly what he expressed to the friars in the *Rule*.

---

[147] SK 461

He recommended mutual, fraternal love in these words: *"If a mother cherishes and loves the son that is born to her, how much more deeply one should love and cherish his spiritual brother!"*[148] In his *Rule for life in the hermitages*, he ordained that two of the friars *"be mothers"* to the one or two friar hermits.[149] In the *Legend of the Three Companions* it is written, in fact, how from the beginning the friars in the communities of the Minors "loved one another with profound affection, and they served one another and procured what was necessary, just as a mother would do in her tender love for her only son."[150]

What about St. Francis of Assisi's own conduct? The Seraphic Doctor St. Bonaventure in his *Major Life* wrote that the Seraphic Father nourished an ardent love "towards souls, redeemed by the precious blood of Christ Jesus; and when he saw them sullied by the ugliness of sin, he would weep with such tender pity that he would give birth to them in Christ each day like a mother."[151] We can only imagine how much more St. Francis *gave birth in Christ* to his friars *"like a mother."*

When he wanted to obtain the Pope's approbation of the Rule of the new religious Order of the Friars Minor, the Seraphic Father presented himself to the Pope by portraying himself as *"a poor and very beautiful lady"* who lived in the desert and had become the bride of *"a great king"* by whom she gave birth to *"many beautiful children."*[152] Yet again, in the *Legend of the Three Companions* we read of a vision in which St. Francis of Assisi sees himself as a mother, represented in a significant, evangelical manner (cf. Mt 23:37), by way of the figure of a *"mother hen"* who had "such a quantity of chicks that she was unable to bring them all together under her wings." The Saint said that this was true from the moment in which "the Lord, in His mercy, gave me and will give me many children which I am not able to protect with my own strength alone…"[153]

We should not be surprised, therefore, if the *Franciscan Sources* inform us that St. Francis considered himself a "mother" to his friars[154] and that the friars themselves

---

[148] *Rule of 1223*, Ch. VI (FF 91).
[149] *Religious Life in Hermitages* (FF 136).
[150] The *Legend of the Three Companions*, 41 (FF 1446).
[151] Bonaventure, *Legenda Maior*, Ch. VIII, 1 (FF 1134).
[152] Cf. *Legend of the Three Companions*, 50; Celano, *Second Life of St. Francis*, 16; Bonaventure, *Legenda Maior*, Ch. III, 10 (FF 1459; 602; 1064).
[153] *Legend of the Three Companions*, 63 (FF 1477).
[154] *Letter to Brother Leo* (cf. FF 250).

sometimes addressed St. Francis as *"mother"* or *"tender mother."*[155] Br. Pacificus, in fact, once addressed St. Francis with the expression *"most dear mother."*[156] What, then, must have been the particular atmosphere of the *fraternal life* in the first communities where St. Francis was able to be present with his *spiritual motherhood* which conformed him so radically to the divine Mother that he was expressly called *"most dear mother"*?

From this source, namely the invaluable presence of *"a mother's heart"*[157] in the Seraphic Father, one can rightly speak of that extraordinary *Marian* dimension of Franciscanism which rests at the *heart* of Franciscan Christocentrism. This has been passed on through the centuries in the Franciscan Order and will continue until the end of time. In this uninterrupted Franciscan school were some of the greatest Marian voices such as St. Anthony of Padua, St. Bonaventure of Bagnoregio, Bl. John Duns Scotus, St. Bernardine of Siena, St. Lawrence of Brindisi, and St. Leonard of Port Maurice. The list of other Saints, Blesseds, and Venerables of the Seraphic Order continues right up to St. Maximilian Mary Kolbe, apostle and martyr of the Immaculate in the twentieth century.

"Motherhood" in St. Maximilian

In the life of St. Maximilian this active and fervent presence, *Marian* at root and *maternal* in character, was no less consistent. Obviously, this presence should not be lacking in anyone who is consecrated without limits to the Immaculate, especially those who are consecrated with the *Marian Vow* and even more so those who live in a community where all are consecrated with the *Marian Vow*.

This was certainly the case with St. Maximilian himself whose remarkable amiability, and his sweetness of conduct and speech, was recognized by all. The friars at the *Niepokalanòw* in Poland and the one in Japan felt themselves to be true "children" of St. Maximilian. They considered him both a *"father and mother."*

---

[155] Cronicles and Other Franciscan Testimonies, *Br. Thomas the Tuscan*, 1 (FF 2677).
[156] Celano, *Second Life of St. Francis*, 137 (FF 721).
[157] Bonaventure, *Legenda Minor*, St. Francis' Outstanding Virtues, 8th Les. (FF 1354).

Just from St. Maximilian's letters alone there is ample evidence of this and the citations could be multiplied, but the two below taken from his letters should be sufficient.

In the first letter he writes to the friars that the Immaculate *"has communicated to me such a tenderness and love towards all of you (both in Japan and Poland), truly similar to the tenderness that a dad or mom has towards their beloved son. And this is even in conformity with the spirit of the first centuries of our Order when the superior was called mother."*[158]

In the second letter he writes in this way: *"My dear ones, St. Paul in his letter to the Corinthians (or another, I can't remember) says more or less the following: 'Even if you had 10,000 teachers in Christ, you did not have many fathers because I was the one who brought you forth in Christ'* [cf. I Cor 4:15]. *I too, therefore, joyfully apply this to myself, rejoicing in the fact that the Immaculate has deigned, in spite of my miseries, weaknesses, stupidity, and unworthiness, to pour into you Her life through me, to make of me your* mother."[159]

No less interesting and meaningful are the many testimonies about the *maternal* dimension of St. Maximilian's sentiments. Though the brothers themselves left numerous accounts, we will only report a few here.[160]

Fra Juraszek recalls: At *Niepokalanòw* "I slept in the bed next to his for some time. One time I woke up in the middle of the night because I suddenly realized that someone was sweetly covering my feet. I opened my eyes and… what did I see? It was Fr. Maximilian! Every time I recall this episode tears come to my eyes. He seemed to be infinitely sensitive, just as the most tender of mothers could have been" (p.110).

Fra Pelagio Poplawski remembers: "At one time I fell into a deep depression which lasted about three months, and Fr. Maximilian was like a mother to me. Unhappy and downtrodden as I was, he comforted my spirit and tended to me with the tenderness of a mother. I am indebted to him for having gotten through that situation" (p.120).

---

[158] SK 328
[159] SK 503
[160] Cf. Patricia Treece, *A Man for Others. Maximilian Kolbe, the Saint of Auschwitz.*

Fr. Corrado Szweda, who was a prisoner with St. Maximilian at Auschwitz, recalls: "When I had finished my work shift and went to him he would take my head and place it on his chest, just as a mother does her son. [...] I owe a great deal to his motherly heart" (p.179).

In living the *Marian Vow*, then, the fraternal life of the religious community must be animated with an intense love for the Immaculate. This cannot help but reflect itself outwardly. It shows itself in the interpersonal relationships as that sweet and delicate Marian dimension which is totally *maternal* in sentiment. So be it, always, for our communities!

"Motherhood" in St. Clare

Obviously this "maternal" dimension is present in an even more evident manner in St. Clare of Assisi. In her *Rule* there is applied to the nuns the exact same passage of St. Francis' Rule: *"If a mother loves and nourishes the daughter that is born to her, how much more deeply one should love and cherish her spiritual sister!"* [161] In her *Testament* she writes that the Abbess of each monastery should be *"like a good mother towards her daughters."* [162] Indeed, she expressly defined herself *"your mother and servant"* [163] and, again, *"your sister and mother."* [164]

In one of her *Letters* St. Clare writes to St. Agnes of Prague and speaks of that *"fire of love toward you,"* a fire of love that is *"ardent and sweet in the heart of your mother."* [165] She humbly recommends to St. Agnes: *"may you remember your poor mother."* [166]

The Supreme Pontiff himself, in his *Bull of Canonization*, defines the Saint as that *"Mother fruitful in all of the virtues."* [167]

In the *Legend of St. Clare* there are a large number of texts which speak of St. Clare's "motherhood." We cite but one of the most beautiful and meaningful passages.

"Not only did this venerable Abbess love the souls of her daughters, but she took care even of their bodies with the astonishing zeal of

---

[161] St. Clare, *Rule*, Ch. VIII (FF 2798).
[162] (St. Clare)*Testament* (FF 2848).
[163] Ibid., (FF 2853).
[164] St. Clare, *Blessing* (FF 2855).
[165] St. Clare, *Letters* (FF 2900).
[166] Ibid., (FF 2907).
[167] (St. Clare) *Process of Canonization* (FF 3311).

charity. *Indeed, in the cold of the night she very often would cover them up with her own hands when they were sleeping; and she desired that those whom she saw were incapable of observing the common austerity might follow a less severe regiment. If anyone was disturbed by temptation, or, as can happen, if any were sad, she would call them aside and, weeping, would console them. Sometimes she would prostrate herself at the feet of the afflicted in order to alleviate the violence of their pain with her motherly caresses.*"[168] *"And her daughters, not ungrateful for her acts of goodness, paid her back with total dedication. They accepted her affectionate love of a mother..."*[169]

"Motherhood" in St. Veronica Giuliani

No less exemplary was the "maternal" dimension which was present and operative in St. Veronica Giuliani, the Capuchin Poor Clare mystic who bore the stigmata. In many pages of her *Diario* she points out her commitment to conduct herself *"as a true mother, with that zeal and spirit of accomplishing and doing everything that the Rule commands."*[170]

In the *Testimonies* for the *Process of Canonization* we read how, as the Novice Mistress, St. Veronica attended to each novice with great charity and a totally *maternal* attention. She showed them "a holy *tenderness* in their every spiritual, yes, and temporal need" (according to the testimony of Bl. Florida Cevoli). Sr. Clare Felice attests that the Saint opened her entire heart to her novices, "instructing them with such goodness and charity that they adored her and *called her their mother*. Like a mother she was full of charity and without even being asked by them she would come to their every need."

If her charity was always great towards her sisters, then she became even more caring towards the sick sisters as many testimonies confirm. Like a *loving mother* St. Veronica, Abbess of the Monastery, put herself to every domestic task, even the most abject; she even would take the place of the extern or lay nuns [who did more manual work and weren't among the choir nuns who chanted the Divine Office], especially when these were "sick, when she never abandoned

---

[168] Celano, *Legend of St. Clare* (FF 3233).
[169] Ibid., (FF 3234).
[170] Vol. VI, pp. 273–274.

them in their infirmities and came to their aid with admirable charity" (as Bl. Florida Cevoli again gives witness).

It is also important to reflect upon St. Veronica's spirit which seemed to feel the agitation of the entire world with all of its concerns. She demonstrated that in the cloister one's heart does not close itself off, but rather opens itself up and knows how to lovingly take into view the widest horizons, namely the horizons of divine charity which were the horizons of Our Lady's universal motherhood.

St. Veronica treated those who helped the monastery with the same maternal charity, particularly agents or farmers, and wished that they be repaid. If she was great and tireless in her charity towards the nuns, "coming to their aid as a true *mother* in all of their needs both spiritual and temporal," she was equally so towards the extern sisters and the servants of the monastery whom she wanted to be "punctually assisted and satisfied."[171]

---

[171] To see all of the testimonies, cf. *Tifernaten. Beatificationis et Canonizationis ven. Servae Dei Sor. Veronicae de Iilianis… Summarium super dubio.* Rome 1762.

CHAPTER 7
THE MARIAN VOW: THE LIFE OF UNION WITH THE IMMACULATE

The "presence" of the Immaculate, therefore, particularly with regard to Her children who have made the *Marian Vow*—and still more so for a "religious community" with the *Marian Vow*—cannot but be a "presence" of the most authentic and concrete possession. It is a mystical-supernatural "presence"; one which is not merely a "presence" of knowledge or affectivity (*in distans,* as happens in nature), but rather a proximate "presence" which could be said to be personal-corporal, albeit ever invisible, as the mystical experiences of many of the Saints teach us. It is a "presence" which, in substance, is *analogous* to that of Our Lady to Her Firstborn Son, Jesus, when She lived at Nazareth during Her earthly life. Indeed, we can rightly believe that Her "presence," although invisible to us, *really and mystically* prolongs that same "maternal presence" She gave to Jesus, Her divine and Firstborn Son, during Her earthly sojourn, above all at Nazareth, and the same "presence" She proffered to St. Joseph, Her virgin Bridegroom, who was so deeply united to Her.

The Blessed Virgin Herself explains this beautifully and exquisitely to St. Gertrude in an apparition where She says, "My sweetest Jesus is not only *unigenitus*, my only child, but *primogenitus*, my Firstborn, because I conceived Him first in my womb, but after Him, or better in Him, I conceived all of you within my motherly love so that you might be simultaneously His brothers and my children."

Consequently, the divine Mother who was *really* "present" to Her Firstborn cannot but be *really and mystically* "present" to Her second-born, third-born, fourth-born, etc. And it is from this "presence," as from a spring, that there flows the life of union with the Immaculate. We are speaking here, especially for those with the *Marian Vow*, of a concrete life of union which makes perceptible the real "presence" of the Immaculate. This "presence" is perceived both internally and externally by way of the spiritual senses; that is, with the *"eyes of the heart"* as St. Paul efficaciously explains and many Saints through the centuries attest.

ST. MAXIMILIAN M. KOLBE

We have two testimonies which are very close to us from the 20th century in the life and doctrine of St. Maximilian M. Kolbe and that of St. Pio of Pietrelcina who are our Patron Saints and models, together with our Seraphic Father St. Francis and Holy Mother St. Clare of Assisi.

St. Maximilian M. Kolbe (†1941) has left us a testimony of the life of union with the Immaculate which began during his exceptional childhood. What a witness this is, since as a ten-year-old boy he had the extraordinary experience of having an apparition of Our Lady who presented "two crowns" to him, one white and the other red. One represented his virginal, consecrated life and the other, his bloody martyrdom, to both of which he was called. This event characterized his entire life with Her "presence" which became ever more fervent and intense. He even arrived at the point of constantly *"breathing"* the Immaculate, of having Her as his *"fixed idea,"* and of entering into that *"mad love"* for Her.

St. Maximilian showed in a living manner his authentic self-donation to Her by his *"feverish action"* for Her cause and the coming of the Kingdom of Christ in the world. He aspired to live always with Her and entirely for Her, without sparing or reserving anything. Hence, he would not allow himself to rest and he employed all of his powers to bring the Immaculate everywhere and make Her "present" as much as he possibly could in every home, family, town, and city. He passionately desired to make Her "present" in the hearts of all men *"who now live and shall live in the future."*[172]

We should hold for certain that St. Maximilian continually lived alongside the Immaculate; that he truly saw Her *"with the eyes of the heart"* as St. Paul says (Eph 1:18). He remained always near to Her in accord with his pledge of unlimited consecration. She, for Her part, inspired him to *"live, work, suffer, be consumed, and die"* for Her, only for Her, and thus to accomplish deeds both great and small. Some of his undertakings were unreal—truly unbelievable and, humanly

---

[172] SK 1325

speaking, impossible! Such was the case with the foundation of the two Cities of the Immaculate in Poland and Japan and with that Marian editorial development intended to envelop the entire globe with Marian literature.

In reality the whole fruitfulness of St. Maximilian's apostolic action flowed precisely from the wellspring of his constant union with the Immaculate. He himself came to say, in fact, *"Union with the Immaculate, to be an instrument in Her Immaculate hands: here is the secret which guarantees success."*[173] Hence, he never grew weary of offering this recommendation: *"We must belong to Her under every aspect; we must be Hers in the strictest and most perfect way possible; we must be, in a certain sense, She Herself."*[174] He also surpassed this when he wrote that we must commit ourselves in such a way that *"She might more and more take possession of our soul, that She might appropriate it totally to Herself and She Herself might think, speak, love God and neighbor, and act in and through it."*[175]

SAINT PIO OF PIETRELCINA

St. Pio of Pietrelcina (†1968) was born in the month of Mary (May 25, 1887) and baptized at the baptismal font of the Church of St. Mary of the Angels in Pietrelcina. He lived almost his entire priestly life at the Friary and Sanctuary of the *Madonna delle Grazie* (Our Lady of Graces) in San Giovanni Rotondo. He was bound to Our Lady above all by his Rosary beads, a devotion he learned well from the example of his dear and pious mother. Indeed, he came to recite the Holy Rosary day and night in a truly extraordinary manner.

Thus, the "presence" of Our Lady in St. Pio's long life as a Capuchin Franciscan was effectively represented by the external *sign* of his Rosary, both the one which hung from his cord about the waist and the one which he kept in his hand in order to continually thumb his beads. He even reached the point of saying over a hundred Rosaries a day—an exceptional mystical gift which has perhaps never had its equal in any of the Saints in two thousand years of hagiography.

---

[173] SK 1071
[174] SK 634
[175] SK 1211

Moreover, the "presence" of the Madonna filled up the entire interior life of Padre Pio. He himself, in fact, wrote that his mystical life of union with Jesus was entirely due to Her: *"I feel tightly-knit and close to the Son by means of this Mother without even seeing the chains which keep me bound."* Nor did he hide the fact of Our Lady's "presence" at his side, but rather expressly confirmed it with all simplicity saying, *"The Madonna… is always with me,"* or attesting to the fact that She was always "present" in his cell. She was even more "present" at his side at the altar during the Holy Mass. This was true also during the numerous hours each day when he administered the Sacrament of Confession when he would see "the penitent accompanied by the hand of Mary Most Holy to his confessional, like a naughty child led to school by his mother!"[176]

UNION BETWEEN THE MOTHER AND HER CHILDREN

Following the school of the Saints, especially learning from their experiences and teaching, it is not hard for us to grasp that the life of union with Mary in its very nature is characterized by a life of union between the Mother and Her children. This acquires all the more consistency for us because of the *Marian Vow* of unlimited consecration which makes us belong to the Immaculate. The *Marian Vow* is so complete and radical that it constitutes us as the *"absolute property"* of the Immaculate and encloses us in Her womb so as to be *christified* in and by Her in the most sublime way possible. This was the teaching of St. Maximilian who briefly, yet concisely explained: *"in the womb of the Immaculate the soul is reborn in the form of Jesus Christ."*[177]

After His birth, the Infant Jesus was nursed, reared, and formed by His divine Mother up until His adult years. Therefore, if our soul is mystically reborn of Our Lady in the form of Jesus Christ, then clearly it must be nursed and fed by Her in order to grow unto *"perfect manhood, to the mature measure of the fullness of Christ"* (Eph 4:13).

Indeed, St. Maximilian writes, *"She has to nourish the soul with the milk of Her grace, lovingly take care of it and educate it just as She nourished, cared for, and educated Jesus. The soul must learn to know and love Jesus on Her knees. It must draw love for Him from Her Heart, or*

---

[176] Cf. *Padre Pio parla della Madonna*, p.92.
[177] SK 1295

even love Him with Her Heart and become like unto Him by means of love."[178]

Elsewhere the Saint writes, *"My dearly beloved children in the Immaculate, I congratulate you on being nourished by Her very person with the milk of Her graces, caressed by Her, and formed by Her just as She did with Jesus, our elder Brother, so that the divine Bridegroom of our souls might recognize in us ever more and more the very same features which He received from the Immaculate, His Mother, those same eyes, that same little heart."*[179]

Again the Saint writes, *"As Christ, the source of graces, became Her property, so too does the distribution of graces belong to Her. Every grace is the fruit of the life of the Most Holy Trinity: the Father generates the Son from all eternity, while the Holy Spirit proceeds from Them both [...]. The Holy Spirit who proceeds from all eternity from the Father and the Son, by means of this grace forms souls in and through the Immaculate unto the likeness of the Firstborn, the God-Man."*[180]

"Let us turn our gaze to Jesus, our most perfect Model," St. Maximilian reflects in another place. *"He, God, holiness itself, gave Himself to the Immaculate without any reserve; He became Her child; He desired that She guide Him according to Her own good pleasure for a good thirty years of His earthly life. Do we perhaps need a better encouragement?"*[181]

Therefore, in an entirely mystical key which was Marian, Christian, and Trinitarian, he was able to decisively sum up everything by writing, *"She alone must instruct each one of us in every moment; She must lead us, transform us into Herself, in such wise that it is no longer we who live, but She in us, just as Jesus lives in Her and the Father in the Son. Let us allow Her to do with us and by means of us whatever She desires and surely She will accomplish miracles of grace: we will become saints and great saints…"*[182]

> It is interesting to note how St. Louis M. Grignion de Montfort had already preceded St. Maximilian in describing Mary's totally maternal action in regards to Jesus. This was how Jesus willed it for Himself according to the divine design.

---

[178] Ibid.
[179] SK 461
[180] SK 1296
[181] SK 1232
[182] SK 556

Indeed, Jesus *"glorified His independence and majesty,"* St. Louis de Montfort writes, *"by depending upon this amiable Virgin in His conception, His birth, His presentation in the Temple, His hidden life for thirty years, and even at His death where She had to assist Him, in order to accomplish in Her the one and the same sacrifice, and be immolated by Her consent to the eternal Father [...].*

"She nursed Him, fed Him, kept Him, reared Him, and sacrificed Him for us. O what admirable and incomprehensible dependence of a God which the Holy Spirit was unable to pass over in silence in the Gospel [...].

"Jesus Christ gave more glory to the Father by His submission to His Mother for thirty years than what He could have done by converting the whole world with the most spectacular miracles. Oh! How greatly we glorify God when, in order to please Him, we submit ourselves to Mary based on the example of Jesus Christ, our sole Model!"[183]

IMITATE JESUS IN EVERYTHING

In all truth the whole life of Jesus upon this earth was a life of continuous and intimate union with His divine Mother. From His virginal conception in the womb of the Immaculate and His virginal birth in the Grotto of Bethlehem, the entire life and growth of Jesus *"in wisdom and age and grace"* (Lk 2:52) was realized through the divine Mother's love and assistance year after year. He lived thirty years almost exclusively at Nazareth followed by the brief period of His public life. Since Jesus is the *"firstborn of many brethren"* (Rm 8:29), it is certain that the spiritual journey and the life of grace for all of Jesus' lesser brothers can be gathered from those thirty years of continuous union between the Mother and the Son, since His brethren are also Mary's children—She being their *"Mother in the order of grace"* (LG 61).

Ven. Fr. Gabriel M. Allegra spoke well when he synthesized this fact with enlightened simplicity: *"For me the spiritual life is the simplest thing in this world: it consists solely in living with Our Lady,*

---

[183] *True Devotion*, n.18.

like Jesus-Love." Jesus is infinite perfection. Hence, imitating Jesus by living always with Our Lady as He did, by uniting ourselves to Her in total love and subjecting ourselves to Her in obedient love for the whole of our lives, means to travel the most perfect itinerary of the spiritual life for the fullest and most sublime holiness.

St. Louis de Montfort had earlier written, with great clarity, that looking to Jesus and *"having before our eyes such an example, so visible and known to all, would we not be foolish to think we could find a more perfect and suitable means for glorifying God than that of submitting ourselves to Mary after the example of Her Son?"*[184]

This is exactly what should be realized with the *Marian Vow* of unlimited consecration to the Immaculate. In its essence and simplicity the *Marian Vow* is the life of total dedication to the Immaculate with the bond of belonging to Her in a special way as Her *"absolute property"* in complete dependence upon Her and in full obedience of love for Her: exactly like Jesus!

ARRIVING AT IDENTIFICATION

Moreover, we should take note that the life of union with the Immaculate realized and lived out fully with the *Marian Vow* cannot but bring us to the most intimate and profound union of love with Her. This union becomes a fusion of love and brings about our *transubstantiation* into the Immaculate to the point of an *identification* with Her. Hence, as St. Maximilian so succinctly puts it, there comes a point where *"She alone,"* the Immaculate, lives in us and we in Her; we become, in a certain sense, *"another Mary living, speaking, and working."*[185]

> This sublime experience of identification with the Madonna can be pondered, in fact, in the conclusion to the life of St. Clare of Assisi as described and recorded in the testimonies of the Process of her Canonization.[186]
>
> St. Clare was already near to her passage from this world to the Kingdom of Heaven. The nuns were lovingly and continually assisting her in her last days. And one of the nuns had an admirable vision of a procession of glorious

---

[184] *True Devotion*, n.139.
[185] SK 486
[186] Cf. (St. Clare) *Process of Canonization* (FF 3083).

virgins who, coming down from Heaven, entered and surrounded the bed upon which St. Clare lay. Among the virgins there was one who was more beautiful, noble, and glorious—it was the Blessed Virgin Mary, crowned with a radiant light that filled the entire room. Drawing near to St. Clare who was lying upon her bed, the Madonna placed Her face near to that of St. Clare, and at that point the nun, looking closely, was unable to distinguish the face of Our Lady from that of St. Clare. The identification was so perfect in appearance that one could not be distinguished from the other!

St. Clare is a supreme example for us. Bl. Thomas of Celano rightly defined her as the "imprint of the Mother of God"[187] and others have called her the "Icon of the Immaculate." Her life, then, is a school where we can learn the complete realization of the *Marian Vow* with all of its fecundity of love and transforming grace in the Immaculate. She accomplished this without even having the grace of taking the *Marian Vow*!

It is up to us who have the *Marian Vow*, therefore, to look to St. Clare and imitate her in living the life of union with the Immaculate. Like St. Clare, our life should be pure, loving, ardent, and faithful to the point of reaching that full identification of love with the Immaculate.

Our Seraphic Father St. Francis, with his *"unspeakable love"* for the Blessed Mother, remains the first master and model of the life of union with Our Lady for those with the *Marian Vow*, just as he was for St. Clare. He never tired of living always united with Her. In fact, he would *"sing special praises in Her honor, lift up prayers, and offer such sentiments that the human tongue is not capable of describing them."*[188]

We must enter, with St. Clare, St. Maximilian, and St. Pio of Pietrelcina, into this school of St. Francis. We must live that life of loving union with Our Lady which immerses us in Her in order that She may purify, transform, and conform us to Jesus Crucified in the holiest and most sublime manner possible.

---

[187] Celano, *Legend of St. Clare* (FF 3153).
[188] Celano, *Second Life of St. Francis* (FF 786).

UNION: 24/7

The life of union with the Immaculate is to be concretely lived out during the entire 24 hours of the day, 7 days a week. This is to be done by exercising the practice of staying under the eyes of the sweet Mother without any interruption and of keeping our own eyes—the *"eyes of the heart"* (Eph 1:18)—always fixed upon Her, upon Her precious presence and nearness, upon Her face so full of motherly love.

If all of the faithful can attain this union "through efforts sustained by grace," as Neubert describes,[189] how much more so those with the commitment of the *Marian Vow*?

It follows, however, that we have to dedicate ourselves to living according to the *Marian Vow* and for this it is particularly necessary to be well habituated in living near the Immaculate in continuous recollection and *"frequent, familiar conversation with Her,"* as St. Maximilian recommends.[190] In this way, we will keep ourselves united to Her in praying, acting, suffering, rejoicing, working, and resting. By continually advancing in this fashion we will create room within ourselves so that She might penetrate our souls and dwell therein, keeping our mind, heart, will, and vigor in Her motherly hands.

Gradually our thinking, loving, acting, working, self-giving, and suffering come to be purified and elevated by Her so as to be transfigured and "dignified" by Her sublime thinking, loving, acting, working, self-giving, and suffering. Oh, to what heights the Immaculate wants to carry Her *"absolute property!"*

Indeed, St. Maximilian splendidly describes this as follows: *"Do you want Her to dwell securely within your soul? Do you desire Her, and only Her, to guide your thoughts and take possession of your whole heart? Do you desire to live totally for Her? If you really desire all of this, then open wide the door of your whole heart before Her and consecrate yourself to Her without any restriction, and this forever... Have you not given thought to what you will become when it is no longer you who act, but She Herself who loves God and men in you and by means of you? Do you not realize that, in such a case, your actions come to be measured by Her dignity? That in Her hands they become pure and without blemish, just as She is all pure and without blemish?"*[191]

---

[189] *Life of Union with Mary*, p. 293.
[190] SK 897
[191] SK 1216

St. Maximilian has left us some very beautiful testimonies about the effects of this life of union with the Immaculate who transforms the friars' souls and manifests Herself in each of their varying lives and in their virtues. The Saint writes, *"It is truly symptomatic that those who have recognized the invitation to consecrate themselves to the Immaculate [...] are usually quite different than others even to the point that they live the Immaculate!"*[192]

And the Saint, thinking and speaking with admiration and joy about the fervor of his friars in loving the Immaculate, was able to write: *"The Immaculate is always penetrating their souls more and more and is always taking possession of their hearts more and more profoundly. Not only is it not necessary to urge them on, but I have to act with great prudence in order to contain their enthusiasm so that their sacrifice may last 'longer'[...]. How can one not sincerely love children such as these? It is evident that the Immaculate has already penetrated these persons in such a way as to make Her goodness and Her love shine through them. Glory to the Immaculate for all that She has deigned to do and will still do in the Niepokalanòw and in the whole world and... in Paradise."*[193]

Twenty-four hours a day: the life of union with the Immaculate for those with the *Marian Vow* must be exactly that. We must never withdraw ourselves from the Immaculate's maternal action of grace because *"She alone,"* St. Maximilian continues, *"must instruct each of us in every instant; She must direct us and transform us into Herself in such wise that it is no longer we who live, but She in us, just as Jesus lives in Her and the Father in the Son."*[194]

UNION WITH OUR LADY...
EVEN UNTO THE EXCHANGE OF PERSONS

This is exactly what happened with St. Veronica Giuliani, the great Capuchin mystic who bore the stigmata. Some of her experiences of the life of union with the Madonna are truly exceptional.

---

[192] SK 383
[193] SK 458
[194] SK 556, 643

CHAPTER 7

It can be said, in fact, that this admirable Saint became ever more the total possession of the Madonna in her life of loving and dolorous union with Her. Hers was a life of union which decisively moved towards pure identification with Mary: an identification so complete that, on Our Lady's part, there came to be even an exchange or substitution of persons between them, without any external change.

This happened several times during the course of St. Veronica's monastic life when she was Abbess of the Capuchin Poor Clare Monastery in Città di Castello. The news of this exchange of persons between the Madonna and St. Veronica has been passed on by Bl. Florida Cevoli, St. Veronica's Vicar, and by the deposition of another nun who was one of the witnesses during the *Process of Beatification and Canonization* of St. Veronica Giuliani. These can be read in the *Summarium* of testimonies for the informative and apostolic Process (reported in: G. Cittadini, *Santa Veronica Giuliani nella luce dei Processi*, 1997). Among these we read:

> "...Sr. Maria Giovanna Maggio recounted the following fact to the judge instructor: 'I also understood from Mother Sr. Florida, the present Abbess, that the Venerable Sr. Veronica was in Hell several times for many hours during the course of one Lent, suffering those pains for the conversion of sinners and during that time when the Venerable was in Hell for the above-said reason the Blessed Virgin took the part of the Abbess appearing under the features of the Venerable Sr. Veronica.'"

Sr. Giovanna Maggio herself referred in her testimony how one time when she herself encountered the Madonna, believing it to be the Abbess (St. Veronica), she was deeply struck by the face, the presence, and the words that were spoken by Our Lady in that encounter with Her under the garments of the Abbess, Sr. Veronica. Sr. Giovanna was so astonished that the Mother Vicar, Bl. Sr. Florida Cevoli, wished to explain what had happened, namely the mystical substitution of St. Veronica's person with that of the Madonna. *"May you know,"* Bl. Florida said, *"that Mother Sr. Veronica is in Hell today suffering for the conversion of poor sinners, and that that which happened to you was through the*

Most Blessed Virgin who appeared as the Mother Abbess Sr. Veronica in taking care of her duties."[195]

This experience is an extraordinary example of the most delectable fruit produced from union with the Immaculate. This complete union becomes so intimate and transforming that it can enable a person to *"become Hers ever more and more,"* as St. Maximilian explains, and this *"in an ever more perfect manner, to make oneself more like unto Her, to become in a certain sense Her, so that She might take possession of our soul ever more completely, [so that She] might rule it totally and, in and through it, She Herself might think, speak, love God and neighbor, and act."*[196]

At this point we can be confident, with and like St. Maximilian, at the prospect of living union with the Immaculate in such a deep way as to be capable of *"breathing Her," "disappearing in Her,"* and even reaching the possibility of *"living eternally of Her spirit."*[197]

---

[195] *Summarium*, p. 40.
[196] SK 1211
[197] SK 614

CHAPTER 8
THE MARIAN VOW AND THE "IMMACULATE HEART"

The *Marian Vow* and Mary's *Immaculate Heart* are like two mountain peaks which come together and unite in the love exchanged between the soul consecrated with the *Marian Vow* and the Immaculate Heart of Mary Most Holy. With the *Marian Vow*, our hearts are bound to that selfsame *"unspeakable love"* with which St. Francis of Assisi[198] surrounded the divine Mother, while the highest love flows from the Immaculate Heart of the divine Mother towards us who, with the *Marian Vow*, have become Her "absolute property."

We must always keep in mind that the *Marian* Vow is the expression of the peak of unreserved, boundless dedication to the Immaculate and that it includes the entire cult of praise and loving veneration towards Her. In Mary's Immaculate Heart, on the other hand, we encounter the peak of motherly love which is so immense as to extend itself as far as creation itself and, in particular, to all mankind which is itself a child of the Immaculate Heart of Mary.

The *Marian Vow* and the *Immaculate Heart* become, when there is a full correspondence between them, a single current of total reciprocal love between our souls and the Immaculate. Adopting a biblical image, we might say that the *Marian Vow* and the *Immaculate Heart* become a veritable *"burning bush"* of love which is ever aflame and never extinguished. This is demonstrated in the example of St. Maximilian M. Kolbe. He really made the Heart of the Immaculate "his own" by living in the Immaculate with a constant, ardent offering of every heartbeat, every breath, every sacrifice, and every prayer to Her. He kept the Immaculate alive within himself as the *"fixed idea"* of his thought, the *"mad love"* of his heart, and the *"feverish action"* of his will.

---

[198] Bonaventure, *Legenda Maior*, (FF 1165).

Knowing the life and example of St. Maximilian, we can rightly say that, by virtue of the *Marian Vow*, we are to be the *"absolute property"* of the Immaculate as he was which means to assimilate ourselves to the Heart of the Immaculate. This assimilation should reach the point that our own heart becomes the Heart of the Immaculate and the Heart of the Immaculate becomes our own heart. Who can comprehend or measure such an ineffable reality of grace?

St. Pio of Pietrelcina, as is well-known, was aflame with such a love for the Madonna that he became all fire in his heart. He himself said that he felt *"a mysterious fire coming from his heart,"* a fire of love so ardent as to constrain him to have *"ice applied to him in order to extinguish so intense a fire."* What, on the other hand, is our heart like?

THE IMMACULATE HEART: THE MYSTERY OF MARY

In its most personal and intimate aspect, the Heart of the Immaculate contains the entire transcendent mystery of Mary. This mystery is expressed by Her ineffable love towards God and neighbor: towards God, Father + Son + Holy Spirit, and towards the Mystical Body of Christ which consists in the Church militant, suffering, and triumphant. This is the plenitude of love in the Immaculate Heart which incommensurably surpasses the love of all the hearts of the Angels, Saints, and men put together.

In two thousand years of Christianity, the Church Fathers and Doctors, the Saints, mystics, apostles, and contemplatives who have meditated upon and written about Mary's Immaculate Heart have been countless. Enkindled by an inextinguishable flame of love, they have sung of the sublime marvels of the Heart of the Immaculate using striking imagery from the Sacred Scripture, poetry, art, and even the beauty of all creation.

> In a brief, but dense synthesis, Ven. Fr. Gabriel M. Allegra writes, *"Summing it all up: the Saints, ecclesiastical Authors, and Mystics have seen in Mary's Heart the Paradise of God, the Eden of the New Adam, the Ark of the Covenant, the heavenly Ladder, the Throne of the Messiah, the holy Temple of God, the Fountain of grace… and therefore they called it: holy Heart, Sacred Heart, brightly refulgent Heart, virginal Heart, maternal Heart, royal*

Heart, most pure Heart, and finally: Immaculate Heart, which seems to me to be the sweetest and most comprehensive title."

Among the great number of Saints, Doctors, and Apostles of the Immaculate Heart of Mary, Ven. Fr. Gabriel recalls some which he rightly holds as *"the greater and more authoritative."* These are *"St. Bernard, St. Anthony of Padua, St. Bernardine of Siena, St. Anthony Mary Claret, and above all, St. John Eudes."*

Among the Supreme Pontiffs who, down through the centuries, have sustained and increased the cult of the Immaculate Heart of Mary we find Pope Clement XIV who, in 1773, approved the Office proper to the *Most Pure Heart of Mary*. His successors, Popes Pius VI and Pius VII, renewed and extended that approbation of the proper Office. And Bl. Pope Pius IX approved more solemnly a new Office and Mass proper to the Immaculate Heart in 1855.

FATIMA AND THE IMMACULATE HEART

With the Fatima apparitions of 1917, the cult of Mary's Immaculate Heart reached its fullest extension and intensity within the Church. The Supreme Pontiff Pius XII, as a matter of fact, solemnly consecrated the entire human race to the Immaculate Heart in 1942.

Since the apparitions, the Immaculate Heart of Mary has come to be more and more understood as containing within itself the entire mystery of Mary and all of the love which God has infused within Her from the beginning: namely, from Her Immaculate Conception with the fullness of grace to the Annunciation with the Incarnation; from Jesus' birth at Bethlehem to the accomplishment of the Redemption-Coredemption during the Crucifixion on Calvary; from Pentecost in the Cenacle to the Assumption of Mary, body and soul, into the Father's House in Paradise.

The Immaculate Heart of Mary is the whole principle and vital wellspring of that saving and sanctifying love for all of humanity in need of salvation and sanctification. Why? Because Her Heart moves and carries everyone to Her divine Son and Savior. Indeed, St. Pio of

Pietrelcina says that *"only the Heart of our heavenly Mother moves and guides us to Jesus."*[199] It is from and by means of the Immaculate Heart of Mary, that "jewel box" containing all graces, that the triumph of Christ's Kingdom will come upon this poor earth profaned as it is by the corruption of man and stained with the blood of his crimes and betrayals.

The most authentic and fundamental teaching on the Immaculate Heart which comes from Fatima cannot but be particularly bound up with the very words of the Blessed Virgin in Her apparitions to the three shepherd children of Fatima: Lucia, Francisco, and Jacinta.

Listen to what Our Lady said about the importance of devotion to the Immaculate Heart on June 13, 1917: *"Jesus wants to make use of you in order to make me known and loved; He wants to establish the devotion to my Immaculate Heart in the world… I will never abandon you: my Immaculate Heart will be your refuge and the way that will lead you to God."*

Our Lady spoke again to the three shepherd children on July 13th after the vision of Hell, saying: *"You have seen where the souls of poor sinners go; in order to save them God wishes to establish the devotion to my Immaculate Heart in the world…"* But if mankind did not convert, Our Lady announced the coming of a second war worse than the first with the diffusion of the darkest errors throughout the world, with persecutions of the Church and the Pope, which would nonetheless be followed by the final triumph of Her Immaculate Heart. Here are Her words: *"In order to stop this* [namely the destruction of war, errors, and persecutions] *I will return to ask for the consecration of Russia to my Immaculate Heart and for the Communion of reparation on the first Saturdays […]. In the end my Immaculate Heart will triumph…"*

> From the little shepherd girls, Jacinta and Lucia, we come to understand more particulars which are no less instructive. Little Jacinta, as a matter of fact, spoke some very significant words to her cousin Lucia who had gone to visit her for the last time just before her death. She said, *"There is but a little time before I go to Heaven, and you are to remain here in order to tell mankind that God wishes to establish devotion to the Immaculate Heart of Mary in the world."*

---

[199] Cf. *Padre Pio parla della Madonna*, p. 192.

Lucia of Fatima, who has been the primary confidante of the Immaculate Heart, has further made known to us the sweetest predilection and promise made by Our Lady. Mary's words, which are most consoling, were: *"For all those who will honor my Immaculate Heart, I will come to gather them like fragrant flowers at the hour of their death and I will present them before the throne of God."*

Finally, in the third part of the *secret of Fatima*, we see the Angel who is about to set the world ablaze with a fiery sword while the motherly hand of Our Lady intervenes and stops that outburst of fire: the Heart of the Mother always wants to save Her children.

According to Our Lady's message at Fatima, therefore, devotion to the Immaculate Heart is the devotion willed by God, willed by Jesus for the salvation of the world. God wills this devotion to keep sinners from going to Hell, to sanctify devout souls so as to become *"fragrant flowers"* which, at death, will be gathered by the Immaculate Herself and presented by Her *"before the throne of God"* in Paradise.

Hence, it is truly a special devotion which comes to us from Fatima. It can be said that this devotion enters into the very saving designs of God and thus becomes a most powerful and desirable incentive for the salvation of the entire human race.

Ven. Fr. Gabriel writes that the devotion to the Immaculate Heart contained in the message of Fatima "is a luminous, certain, and sweet way, even if it be characterized by martyrdom, which leads to God; in a word, it is the *via Matris* (the way of the Mother), the path trod by the heavenly Mother and indicated by Her to Her children."

Consequently, the words of St. Maximilian addressed to all who are consecrated to the Immaculate, and above all to those who have professed the *Marian Vow*, must be greatly valued. He writes of the Heart of the Immaculate with lively desire, almost in the form of a passionate prayer, *"May She drag all of us to Herself by the hand and press us to Her Immaculate Heart, and each one of us individually, in such wise that we have not the capacity and cannot detach ourselves from Her."*[200]

---

[200] SK 463

IN THE VERY HEART OF THE IMMACULATE

The *Marian Vow*, therefore, is fully linked with the Immaculate Heart and places us on the *Via Matris* or, better still, in the very Heart of the Immaculate. This is because the *Marian Vow* is precisely a vow of the heart, a vow of unlimited love. Everyone who wishes to live out the *Marian Vow* is called and has the grace to root themselves within the Heart of the Immaculate and there to grow spiritually.

In this regard, the expression which St. Maximilian used in speaking of the special grace he had received and was living deep within himself is very significant. He writes, *"The Immaculate has given me hospitality within the home of Her Immaculate Heart."* [201] Clearly we are speaking of a hospitality flowing from a vibrant, ardent love which becomes *transforming* within the very Heart of the Immaculate.

It could also be said, therefore, that the *Marian Vow* not only transubstantiates us into the Immaculate, but even directs us towards transubstantiation into the *very Heart of the Immaculate.* There, in Her Heart, is contained the entire mystery of the person and mission of the Immaculate with all of the graces with which She was filled by God from Her Immaculate Conception and which were later bestowed from the Annunciation until Her Assumption and Coronation in the Kingdom of Heaven.

> In the biblical sense we know that the heart is the seat of the human personality, the seat of the thoughts, affections, passions, and actions of man. Thus, to be transubstantiated into the Immaculate means, after all, to be transubstantiated into the Heart of the Immaculate. Her Heart, writes Ven. Fr. Allegra, is the "summation of all the mysteries, the compendium of all the greatness, all the virtues, all the charisms of the Immaculate Mother."[202]

> And is it not exceedingly beautiful to realize that the Marian Vow, in bringing about the transubstantiation into the Heart of the Immaculate, accomplishes this transformation within the very *Heart of the Immaculate*?

Here we have really come to the very highest peak of the supreme heights of sanctity. Through a mystery of grace and predilection, the

---
[201] SK 440
[202] *Il Cuore Immacolato di Maria, via a Dio*, p. 62.

Immaculate has chosen and called us to this summit through the *Marian Vow*. How do we know this? Because the *Marian Vow* is a vow of the heart, a vow of love. This vow of love aspires to be without measure like the love of the Immaculate; it aspires even to be assimilated to the very Heart of the Immaculate which is the *Sanctuary* of the love of the Father, of the Son, and of the Holy Spirit.

The *Marian Vow* and the *Immaculate Heart*: through reflecting and meditating we will become more aware of the fact and even be able to say that the *Marian Vow* cannot exist without the Immaculate Heart. Indeed, it has its source of being and operating in the Immaculate Heart alone. St. Maximilian writes as follows, *"Behold our ideal: to draw near to Her, to become ever more like Her, to allow Her to take possession of our heart and our entire being, [to allow Her] to live and work in us…"*[203]

It must be stated, therefore, that the *Marian Vow* exists for the Immaculate Heart. When the vow is faithfully lived everyday, it brings us to live not only entirely for and with the Immaculate, but even *in the Immaculate*, and still more *in the very Heart of the Immaculate*, in order to assimilate us and enable us, in the end, to become entirely the *Heart of the Immaculate*.

In the journey of our spiritual growth and interior transformation, the *Marian Vow* demands both the asceticism of the purgative way which brings us to practice the virtues of the Immaculate and the asceticism of the illuminative way which enables us to live like and with the Immaculate. At this point of the spiritual journey, we advance and are able to reach mystical union with the Immaculate by learning how to live *Her in Her,* that is to live ever more profoundly within Her Immaculate Heart which is the *"Dwelling place of the Word and Temple of the Holy Spirit,"* as the Church in our day prays in the *Collect* for the Mass of the *Immaculate Heart of Mary*.

It is precisely here, within the Heart of the Immaculate, that the soul with the *Marian Vow* is, by the loving operation of the Holy Spirit, *transubstantiated* and made immaculate[204] as St. Maximilian teaches.[205] Perhaps we would do well here to recall the splendid words of St. Ambrose, "May Mary's soul be in each of us to magnify

---

[203] SK 1210
[204] *immacolatizzata* in Italian.
[205] SK 531

the Lord," and paraphrase them in this fashion: *"May the Heart of the Immaculate be in each of us to magnify the Lord."*

FUSION AND CHRISTIFICATION

It is certain that here, deep within the womb of the Immaculate Heart, those who are faithful to the *Marian Vow* will achieve the most sublime *christification*. This is so because they come to participate in and to be assimilated to the very *christification* of the Immaculate who is the virginal Mother of Christ, the Incarnate Word, and the Mother of all of those whom She regenerates in Christ as *conformed to Christ*.[206] We do well to repeat once again the quote of St. Maximilian, *"In the womb of the Immaculate the soul is reborn in the form of Jesus Christ"*; and in order to love Jesus the soul *"must draw love for Him from Her Heart, or even love Him with Her Heart and become like unto Him by means of love."*[207]

Regarding this specific point of the *christification* which is accomplished by immersing oneself in the Heart of the Immaculate, Ven. Fr. Gabriel succinctly synthesizes the thought of the great Saint of the Sacred Hearts, St. John Eudes. He writes:

"St. John Eudes contemplates how the admirable Heart of Mary is at the origin of the Mother of God's natural, spiritual, and divine life, and how it is a world of marvels; he considers, secondly, how Mary's Heart is the wellspring and principle of the life of Jesus, the God-Man, which is another, more splendid world of heavenly marvels; he considers, thirdly, that Mary's Heart is at the origin of grace for all the adoptive children in the world and of glory for all of the Blessed in Heaven; therefore, he comes to the conclusion that souls that throw themselves into this Most Pure Heart are transformed into Jesus." And this takes place precisely because Jesus, as St. John Eudes expressly teaches, is the *"divine Heart"* of Mary Most Holy, just as the Holy Spirit is the divine Heart of Jesus.

---

[206] *cristiformi* in Italian.
[207] SK 1295

Ven. Fr. Gabriel confirms this doctrine which is taken from the teaching of many Saints and mystics. Among these there emerges, and rightly so, the following great Saints: St. Bonaventure, St. Bernardine of Siena, St. Lawrence of Brindisi, St. Louis M. Grignion de Montfort, St. Maximilian M. Kolbe, and St. Pio of Pietrelcina.

It follows that when those with the *Marian Vow* throw themselves into the Immaculate's "Most Pure Heart," thus fusing themselves together with Her Heart in a mystical union, they can also be said to be transformed in Jesus, the "divine *Heart*" of Mary. They are therefore most intimately united with Jesus who is Mary's "divine *Heart*."

Thus, there takes place within them a sort of mutual exchange, or osmosis, and a mystical assimilation whereby, as St. Maximilian explains, the Immaculate *"desires to love the divine Heart in them and by means of them to be… they themselves* [that is to say, to take their place] *and make them become Her very self."*[208] In being thus assimilated to Her, they *"will love Jesus with the Heart of the Immaculate."*[209]

St. Maximilian lingers in meditation upon the Sacred Heart of Jesus in its loving rapport with the Immaculate Heart of Mary. With genuine simplicity and brilliance he states that with regards to *"devotion to the Most Sacred Heart of Jesus many stupendous things could be said, for example, about the desire to love the Immaculate with the Heart of Jesus… and to love Jesus with the Heart of the Immaculate."*[210]

JESUS IN THE EUCHARIST—
THE "DIVINE HEART" OF MARY

At this point, we need to reflect upon the fact that Jesus, who lives in Mary and is Her *"divine Heart,"* takes the specific form of Jesus in the Eucharist. In the Eucharist, Jesus is really present with the Body and Blood which He took from the Virgin Mary; in every consecrated Host Jesus is there, living and true, with His Divinity and Humanity. We are speaking of that consecrated Host which the Immaculate always carries in Her breast even in the Kingdom of Heaven above; this we know from the mystical experiences of St. Veronica Giuliani and Bl. Mary Magdalene Martinengo, from the

---
[208] SK 1168
[209] SK 647
[210] SK 654

writings of Venerable Mother Costanza Zauli, and from the image which Ven. Mother Speranza placed upon an altar in the Sanctuary of the Merciful Jesus (Colvalenza, Italy).

The precious supernatural bond which unites those with the *Marian Vow* to both the Immaculate and the Eucharist is totally connatural and profound for two reasons: first, because the "divine Heart" of Mary is Jesus in the Eucharist; second, because of the double transubstantiation, namely, the Eucharistic transubstantiation where the bread and wine are transformed into Jesus' Body and Blood, and the Marian "transubstantiation" where those with the *Marian Vow* are transformed into the "divine Heart" of the Immaculate which is none other than the Eucharistic Jesus.

In this regard, the thought of Sr. Lucia of Fatima is very enlightening. She explains that as *"the bread and wine are converted into the Body and Blood of Christ"* in the Eucharistic consecration, so we *"are absorbed with our vital being into Mary's Heart"* in our Marian consecration.[211]

Precisely because of this, it is obvious that in their vital and loving relationship with the Eucharistic Jesus those who have the *Marian Vow* must, first and foremost, make use of the Immaculate, like a fulcrum, in order to bring the maximum joy to Jesus in the Eucharist in the surest way possible. According to St. Maximilian, we must draw near to Him every time *"by passing through Her, in the same way that Jesus came to us through Her."*[212]

For our instruction, St. Maximilian writes that he who is consecrated to the Immaculate—and all the more so for he who is vowed to Her—*"when he goes to make a visit to Jesus in the Blessed Sacrament, offers the entire visit expressly to the Immaculate, perhaps with the invocation alone of 'Mary,' because he knows that this will procure the greatest pleasure possible for Jesus and also that in such a case it is She who accomplishes the visit in and through him, and that he accomplishes it in and through Her."*[213]

St. Maximilian also states that *"there is no better preparation for Holy Communion than to offer it to the Immaculate [...]. She will prepare our hearts in the best way possible and we will be certain of procuring in this way the greatest joy for Jesus, of manifesting to Him the greatest love."*[214]

---

[211] *'Calls' from the Message of Fatima*, p.127.
[212] SK 643
[213] Ibid.
[214] Ibid.

St. Pio of Pietrelcina recommended that every time we receive Holy Communion we should receive the Eucharistic Jesus into our poor hearts by the hands of the Immaculate. He states, *"When it is She Herself who places Jesus in our hearts, this gives us the right to be Her children, just like Jesus, so that it is impossible for Her to distinguish us from Him."*[215]

If someone *"would desire to procure the greatest joy possible for the Immaculate, according to his strength,"* St. Maximilian recommends that he *"ask to borrow the Most Sacred Heart of Jesus and, in this way, he will be sure to infinitely surpass all mankind and all the angels put together in love towards the Immaculate."* Similarly, by uniting himself to the Heart of the Immaculate in order to love Jesus, it happens that *"he loves Him with Her Heart, or rather, that it is She who in and through him loves Jesus."*[216]

In an attempt to summarize all of this in a few words, it could be said that everything is rooted and centered in the Eucharist. In the Eucharist, Jesus is alive with His Body, Blood, Soul, and Divinity, and it is Jesus who is present in every Eucharistic Tabernacle on earth and in the Tabernacle of the Immaculate Heart of Mary in Paradise for all eternity.

In conclusion, therefore, we are able to comprehend well that when we faithfully live the *Marian Vow*, we advance ever more and more in uniting ourselves to the *"divine Heart"* of the Immaculate which is the Eucharistic Jesus. He is always present in the Heart of the Immaculate, even in the Kingdom of Heaven. The Eucharistic Jesus, visibly the *"divine Heart"* of Mary in Paradise, is, in fact, the "Heart" that is eternally adored by all of the Angels and Saints. So our supreme ideal is precisely that of being *transubstantiated* into the *"divine Heart"* of the Immaculate which is utterly *one*[217] with the Eucharistic Jesus.

---

[215] *Padre Pio parla della Madonna*, p.192.
[216] SK 616
[217] *unificato* in Italian.

CHAPTER 9
THE MARIAN VOW AND THE APOSTOLIC LIFE

Besides the missionary call *ad gentes*, which is a specific characteristic of the *Marian Vow*, so too, all of our apostolic activity, even the most ordinary, in our own neighborhoods and Churches certainly falls within the ambit of the *Marian Vow*. This ordinary activity, in fact, takes on a specific character with the *Marian Vow* which is ever valid and beautiful: namely, that *Marian character*, specifically bound to the *universal Immaculate Mediatrix*, who is inseparable from the entirely Franciscan *seraphic way of life*.[218]

It goes without saying that the Franciscans of the Immaculate, by virtue of the *Marian Vow*, have the Immaculate Mediatrix of all Graces as the soul and conductor of their apostolate. She always renders fruitful the souls who are faithful in their consecration to Her. Besides carrying the Immaculate Mediatrix to others, they themselves are carried by Her. It is She who animates, sustains, strengthens, and comforts them in all their apostolic activity which is directed towards the salvation of souls for the growth of the Mystical Body, namely, the Church in Heaven and on earth, and directed entirely to the supreme glory of God in time and in eternity.

It is said that one's ideal, for this is its very nature, is present and active in drawing, encouraging, enlightening, guiding, appealing, and sustaining the person in accomplishing a task, especially if it is an arduous one. Martyrs and heroes have always had this explosive wealth of the ideal which animated, sustained, accompanied, and strengthened them to the point that they were made capable of confronting and overcoming death itself in its most dreadful forms.

Well then, the loving and enthusiastic ideal giving light and strength to every Franciscan with the *Marian Vow* for advancing the Kingdom of Christ until its full realization in Heaven and on

---

[218] *seraficità* in Italian.

earth is the Immaculate Mediatrix. Advancing Christ's reign is the saving plan of God and this has become the mission proper to the Immaculate Mediatrix throughout the entire history of salvation. This is the course of man's history and salvation which begins with the *"Woman"* of Genesis 3:15 who crushes the head of the serpent and tempter; it concludes with the *"Woman clothed with the sun"* of Apocalypse 12:1 who defeats the red dragon who is then hurled into eternal flames.

THE MARIAN DIMENSION: ITS SPECIAL VALUE AND IMPORTANCE

The essential Marian dimension of the apostolate in particular has a striking appearance and force which is usually very pleasing to others and very fruitful. This is so because of a double factor: its psychological and theological value.

The *psychological* value of this Marian character comes from the presence of the "feminine" which, received in its highest form, is "motherhood." This paves the way to the hearts of men and penetrates them with such a loving force that only with great difficulty can they resist it. It is the presence of a "Mother!"

This is readily confirmed by recalling the numerous and most celebrated apparitions of Our Lady through the centuries of human history, right up to our own day and age. She has appeared on every continent, and we recall here the most famous places: Guadalupe, Rue de Bac, La Salette, Lourdes, and Fatima. She is the divine, universal Mother who comes and visits Her children in order to call them back to salvation for the coming of the Kingdom of Christ in the battle against the kingdom of Satan.

The *theological* value of this Marian character, moreover, comes from the truth of Faith regarding the Immaculate's universal mediation of grace which She exercises between Christ and mankind. Her mediation is accomplished in a complete unity of love with Her Spouse, the Holy Spirit, and in a perfect symbiosis with the Church since She is the "Virgin made Church," according to the wonderful expression of St. Francis of Assisi. She is the Virgin Mother extended in our Mother, the Church.

Through Her maternal mediation, the Immaculate is, in effect, the one who brings Christ to humanity and who brings humanity to Christ. She is the heavenly "ladder" of Jacob (cf. Gen 28:12) by which Christ came down to men and by which men rise up to God. She always remains the only parent of Jesus, the only one who gives birth to the Savior; She is the only one who gives birth to Jesus in the hearts of men in need of being saved and conducted into the *"Father's House"* (Jn 14:2) which is the Kingdom of Heaven.

Based on this psychological and theological value, so fundamental, true, and incontestable, the Marian apostolate can unfold in all of its fruitful dynamic of grace; and the fruits, as a matter of fact, are very often surprising and extraordinary. The surprising and extraordinary fruits of grace are well-known in the numerous Marian shrines throughout the world. They are truly privileged places for the Church's vitality and through them the Immaculate wishes to draw to Herself all of Her children so as to give them Her Son, the Savior.

WITH EVERY MEANS AVAILABLE, ON THE OFFENSIVE

By virtue of the motherhood and universal mediation of the Immaculate, it is plain that the dynamic of the Marian apostolate must be carried out and extended in all areas of the Church's activity. This means the entire world, the planet earth, in accord with God's saving plan. The Marian apostolate in itself gives an advantage in that its "Marian character" guarantees in a special way the quickest, surest, and easiest way for the salvation and sanctification of souls in Christ.

This is what St. Louis M. Grignion de Montfort and St. Maximilian M. Kolbe taught. The Marian apostolate draws towards and brings about the most rapid, sure, and easy christification of souls by way of their marianization. This is the revealed plan of God as stated by St. Paul who explains that God has *"predestined"* us *"to become conformed to the image of His Son... the firstborn among many brethren"* (Rm 8:29).

It follows, as St. Maximilian points out, that we need *"to introduce the Immaculate into the hearts of all men so that She might erect a throne for Her Son and lead them to know and be inflamed with love for the Most Sacred Heart."*[219] More concretely, St. Maximilian wanted to bring the Immaculate everywhere: into every social reality such as the family home, schools, hospitals, the workplace, factories, offices, universities, art, and entertainment; in a word, into

---
[219] SK 586

every sphere of work or study, including both culture and recreation. Everything looks to Her. In fact, everything is of interest to Her and nothing can be excluded or withdrawn from the saving action of the universal Mediatrix of grace and salvation for each redeemed child of Adam who needs to be led into the Kingdom of Heaven.

How are we to accomplish this? We respond again with St. Maximilian: everything depends, above all, upon our life of union with the Immaculate. The Saint said that to live out our *"union with the Immaculate and to be an instrument in Her immaculate hands: this is the secret which insures success."*[220] It is useless to hope for success and fruitfulness in the apostolate without a close union with the Immaculate. There is nothing so powerful in the apostolate as union with the Immaculate which makes us Her *"absolute property."*

Therefore, St. Maximilian said that *"he who becomes Her property in an evermore perfect manner will, in this way, exercise an ever greater influence in the environment that surrounds him and will inspire others to know the Immaculate more perfectly, to draw ever nearer to Her to the point of becoming She Herself, completely, without any limitation."*[221] In this way, I am able to *"radiate Her so that my environment might be illuminated evermore brightly by knowledge of Her, heated and inflamed evermore ardently by love for Her."*[222]

It is upon this foundation of a most intense life of union with the Immaculate that we need, therefore, to act and commit ourselves in the active apostolate. In our apostolic labors we must make use of every licit means, without exception, from the smallest, most simple to the greatest, most sophisticated. These means presuppose, of course, the spiritual and supernatural means which always must have the first place, and this *in an absolute sense,* such as incessant prayer, the Sacraments, generous penance, and that good example, which must never be lacking, of the practice of the Christian virtues and dedication to work without sparing any efforts.

The Marian apostolate demanded by the *Marian Vow* is, moreover, global and confrontational; it is active and bellicose; it is directed towards conquering, and therefore it must take to the offensive. It cannot content itself with remaining only on the defensive and simply guarding the good which is already possessed. Guarding and defending do not expand nor advance the range of

---

[220] SK 1071
[221] SK 1211
[222] SK 1231

the Kingdom of God; they do not push towards conquering the buttresses and positions of Satan who is ruling in paganism.

"We are on the offensive," St. Maximilian said, *"defending religion is too little for us; rather we are leaving the fortress and, confident in our Leader, going among the enemies and hunting for hearts in order to vanquish them for the Immaculate [...] Every heart which beats upon the earth and which shall beat, until the end of the world, must be prey for the Immaculate: this is our purpose. And this as soon as possible."*[223]

For those with the *Marian Vow*, therefore, the apostolate is a militant apostolate with capillary and massive strategic action according to the needs which are most pressing and activities which are most useful in the present moment. It makes use of the individual, but also organizes collectively in circles or groups of apostolic commitment according to the various fields of interest and activity: missionary work, in-depth doctrinal study, dedication to spiritual retreats, works of charity, the Catholic press, art, entertainment, etc.

If it is true, and it is true indeed, that Satan's kingdom, with all of its heavily armed squadrons of servants spread throughout the world, is always actively assaulting the Kingdom of Christ, then the exhortation of St. Maximilian is most important, especially for us who are *vowed* to the Immaculate: *"Let us get to work!"*[224] Let us try not to forget these burning words of apostolic zeal: *"Is it licit, before the very harsh attacks of the enemies of the Church of God, to remain inactive? Is it perhaps licit for us just to lament and shed tears? Absolutely not. Let us remember that at the judgment seat of God we shall give a strict account not only of the actions we have accomplished, but God will include on the balance also all of the good actions which we could have done, but in reality have transgressed. There is a most holy burden upon each one of us to place ourselves in the trenches and to drive back the attacks of the enemy with our own chest."*[225]

Among the many writings of St. Maximilian, the following is certainly exceptional. He presents the outline of the strategic plan of attack and apostolic conquest which bound the large community of friars in the City of the Immaculate, *Niepokalanòw*. He writes: *"Our community has a lifestyle that is a bit heroic; Niepokalanòw is and must be like that if it really wishes to follow the purpose it is aimed at, that is not only to defend the Faith, to contribute towards the salvation*

---
[223] SK 206
[224] SK 1019
[225] SK 1023

of souls, but to enter into the heated battle without regard for ourselves in order to conquer one soul after another for the Immaculate, conquering one outpost after another, hoisting Her banner above editorial buildings of the daily, periodical and occasional publications, of the printing offices, the radio antennas, the filming rooms, the parliaments, senates, in a word everywhere upon the earth; and more, to be vigilant so that no one may succeed in removing these banners."[226]

MASS MEDIA: THE CHOICE OF PREFERENCE

The choice of means and methods to be used for the apostolate is obviously made according to the present demands in a given location, responding to the most pressing emergencies and necessities. The selection is to be made with a view to the greater good as charity and prudence suggest, and this always in harmony, to the degree possible, with the pastoral plans of the Church which take the pulse, as it were, of the People of God and know the most urgent needs for the salvation of souls.

> The primary and preferential choice, at any rate, could and even should be that of the apostolic use of the *mass media* (press, radio, television, audio and video productions, and the internet). The mass media has a great power of diffusion and a wide range, even global (via satellite and internet), of direct and immediate contact with souls, both individually and collectively among the People of God, who need to be evangelized and saved.

> The unlimited apostolic efforts to give the Immaculate to the whole of humanity on the part of the religious family of the Franciscans of the Immaculate, with the assistance of the lay Missionaries of the Immaculate Mediatrix, must continue along these lines. The goal is to cover entire regions, nations, and even "via satellite and via internet" all of the continents in the world with collected works, books, studies, leaflets, periodicals, and magazines—written and possibly translated into various foreign languages—and with the establishment of radio and television stations in every possible location.

[226] SK 199

It goes without saying that we are speaking of continuous and tireless efforts. These efforts are focused on evangelizing the whole of humanity with the truth that comes from God. The Gospel must radiate to every man by means of the printed word, images and audio (via airwaves), so as to enlighten him and give She Herself who in turn gives birth to Jesus, the one and only divine Savior of all, in his heart.

STUDYING AND SPEAKING LANGUAGES

In particular there must be efforts to know the most commonly spoken languages which are used in the world. This effort is very important and it must be done because we must make St. Maximilian's commitment our own. He wrote, *"We desire to speak to every soul that is living upon the earth and in every language [...]. With the passing of time, we desire not to transgress any of the languages which are more commonly spoken in the world."*[227]

With regards, then, to the content of Marian preaching, it is an absolute duty and necessity to make the Immaculate known and loved. This is to be done by word and action using graphics and the airwaves. She is to be preached in all Her mysterious reality— integral and intact—according to revelation which comes to us from Sacred Scripture and Tradition, the Liturgy, the Papal Magisterium, the school of the Saints (especially the Franciscan Saints), and from the most genuine *sensus fidelium*.

This is absolutely necessary given the confusion of ideas in which we find ourselves today. The present situation is reducing mankind and Christians themselves to painful and dangerous conditions through a merciless relativism, syncretism, irenicism, and false ecumenism. These deprive people of the necessary foundations and secure references for the life of faith.

All passing hypotheses and novelties are, therefore, forbidden and placed under the ban. Unfortunately these always find *"itching ears"* (2 Tim 4:3). Also under the ban are all of the old and new errors, especially those which, at present, are deforming the ineffable mystery of our divine Mother and Queen in Her most important and beautiful prerogatives and privileges (*the Immaculate Conception,*

---

[227] SK 880

divine Maternity, perpetual Virginity, Coredemption, Mediation, Assumption, and *Queenship*).

Every Franciscan of the Immaculate, in virtue of the *Marian Vow*, must not only be enamored of Our Lady, but must become an expert on Our Lady according to the means available. This expertise must be on all levels: study, doctrine, technology, science; and this according to the measure of the task which is assigned for the teaching and guiding of others. He must know thoroughly how to refute every doctrinal error.

But if this work of teaching the truth about the mystery of Mary and the technical efforts to transmit it are to have that indispensable fecundity, we must first tend to the responsibility of being an expert on Our Lady at the level of the spiritual life with Marian piety, cult, and ardent devotion. Our entire spiritual family is called to this expertise by vocation and mission.

"TO LEAD THE ENTIRE WORLD TO YOU"

In conclusion, let us say that in substance we, as Franciscans of the Immaculate, must daily live out our consecration to the Immaculate with radical commitment in the spirit St. Maximilian who, in an ardent act of consecration, wrote: *"Grant that I might praise You, O Most Holy Virgin, by my personal commitment and sacrifice. Grant that I might live, work, suffer, be consumed, and die for You, only for You."*[228]

We must particularly aspire, each of us outdoing the other, to give an ever new and greater glory to the Immaculate as St. Maximilian's passionate prayer goes on to say: *"Grant that I might give You such glory that no one up to now has ever offered You. Grant that others may surpass me in zeal for Your exaltation, and that I might surpass them, so that by way of such a noble rivalry Your glory may increase ever more profoundly, ever more rapidly, ever more intensely, as He desires, He who has exalted You above all other beings in such an ineffable manner."*[229]

In virtue of this ardent prayer, who could ever hold back the fervent impulse of the Friar, Sister, Poor Clare, Tertiary, or Missionary of the Immaculate Mediatrix in his or her burning personal devotion and generous commitment to the Marian apostolate which must be accomplished in every form and every location possible?

---

[228] SK 1305
[229] Ibid.

There is, however, yet another invocation in the prayer of St. Maximilian which, in the end, is truly enormous. It seems that it is the most demanding and goes beyond all human limits. It is an expression filled with the apostolic and missionary character of consecration to the Immaculate and that uncontainable anxiety of a heart which is so great as to go out to the whole world—just as it should be for each one of us by virtue of the *Marian Vow*. The invocation of St. Maximilian is this: *"Grant that I might lead the entire world to You."*[230]

This must be the *motto* for our entire family as Franciscans of the Immaculate and for each of us individually: *"Grant that I might lead the entire world to You."* This must be the unfurled *flag* of the *Marian Vow* inspiring us to a life of ardent love for the Immaculate, of indefatigable apostolate, and of heroic and profound dedication on the personal level.

The *Marian Vow*, with its apostolic dimension and dynamic, rests entirely upon this goal which envelopes it with the light and force of unlimited love. If lived faithfully through a perfect observance of the *Book of Sanctification*, it cannot help but give to the Church and to all humanity Marian saints and apostles in great number. These Marian souls will be enriched by that fascination of the *"All Beautiful Lady"* (in Latin *Tota Pulchra*), and strengthened by the *"Woman"* who crushes the head of the serpent (Gen 3:15) and defeats the infernal "dragon"—She who is the *"Woman clothed with the sun... and upon her head a crown of twelve stars"* (Apoc 12:1).

> In confirmation of this we have only to think of the undertakings of St. Maximilian. Indeed, he was a Marian apostle dedicated to bringing the Immaculate to the entire world with his burning zeal and ardor of spirit. And was there anything that he did not try to do for Her?
>
> He began by founding a movement which was global in scope: the *Militia Immaculatae*. He founded two Cities of the Immaculate: one in Poland (*Niepokalanòw*), and one in Japan (*Mugenzai No Sono*). In Poland he set up a publishing house with the printing of a Marian review which arrived at one million copies each month, a Marian daily, and other Marian reviews and newspapers. Meanwhile, he had many

---

[230] Ibid.

other grandiose projects in mind and had even written of these, such as:

- the establishment of many Cities of the Immaculate upon the planet earth in all of the continents and nations;

- the establishment of "Marian" radio and television stations;

- the establishment of a "global" Marian review in all of the principal languages;

- the project of training friar pilots for a possible airport at the City of the Immaculate;[231]

- the establishment of the *Immaculatum*, with a huge Marian "library" and "Academy of the Immaculate" for the purpose of the most in-depth study of the ineffable mysteries of the Immaculate Conception and Mary as universal Mediatrix of all graces;[232]

- the establishment of a Marian review in *Latin* for all priests throughout the whole world. And this he actually initiated with the review *Miles Immaculatae* which began in 1938. St. Maximilian hoped to be able "to gather around 'Knights' from the clergy of the whole world and from the candidates for the ecclesiastical state of life."[233]

In the end, St. Maximilian crowned all of his undertakings and aspirations with the most heroic and sublime accomplishment possible in this world: shedding his blood as a martyr. His was martyrdom freely chosen where he generously offered his own life in order to save that of the father of a family condemned to death in the starvation bunker of Auschwitz, that horrendous Nazi concentration and death camp.

Supreme glory to the Saint, Apostle, and Martyr of the Immaculate, luminous model for all those consecrated to the Immaculate with the *Marian Vow!*

---

[231] Cf. SK 778, 786
[232] Cf. SK 508
[233] SK 409; cf. also SK 455, 462

CHAPTER 10
THE MYSTICAL ASCENT OF THE MARIAN VOW

The *Marian Vow* directs us towards and leads us into the mystical life which takes the form of "the mystical life of the Immaculate"; and it cannot, in reality, be other than the very mystical life of the Immaculate. Why? Because the *Marian Vow*, by virtue of its all-absorbing and unifying character, not only unites our soul to the Immaculate, but even desires to assimilate it, transubstantiate it, and therefore unite and identify it with the Immaculate.

We do well to ask: what is the mystical life of the Immaculate? One response in a nutshell is this: the mystical life of the Immaculate is *Her life in Christ* and *His life in Her*, and this through the working of the Holy Spirit who carries Her into the Most Holy Trinity insofar as He unites Her to Christ and immerses Her in the Trinitarian life in the bosom of the Father. We are entering here into the supreme sphere of the infinite!

The Immaculate, the Holy Spirit, the Word Incarnate, the bosom of the Father: this is the *divine ladder* which brings the soul into the Trinitarian life. Every soul redeemed for the Kingdom of Heaven is called to this, starting with St. Joseph, the virgin Spouse of the Immaculate. Since the *Marian Vow* is aimed at assimilating, uniting, and transubstantiating into the Immaculate, it places us precisely upon this *divine ladder* and enables us to climb in the *"briefest, surest and easiest"* way,[234] as St. Maximilian says, so that we may reach the heights of divine perfection.

Transubstantiation into the Immaculate, as a matter of fact, gradually causes the mystical life of the Immaculate to increase in our soul. This occurs by passing through the purifications wrought by the Holy Spirit which are specifically part of the mystical life,

---
[234] SK 542

namely the passive purifications of the spirit, sometimes called the *mystical purgatory* or the *martyrdom of love.*

When passing through these purifications our soul is absolutely powerless to act and thus finds itself in a pure and complete state of *passivity*. The Immaculate, however, is the great specialist in this field. She alone, as a matter of fact, is capable of leading us through these purifications which include the *night of the senses and of the spirit* in order to receive the gift of *infused contemplation.*

The Seraphic Doctor St. Bonaventure sheds great light on the action of the Immaculate in the spiritual life by using the biblical image of the "sun." He writes that "as the sun has purgative, illuminative, perfective, and diffusive virtue, so too does the Blessed Virgin who is completely filled with this fourfold type of supernatural influence."[235]

It can also be said that it is only "through the Immaculate," through Her Heart and motherly hands that the grace of the Holy Spirit radically purifies our nature from sin and elevates it for the experiences of mystical contemplation. This is the high road of *transubstantiation* into the Immaculate which accomplishes in us the most exalted and perfect *christification*. This full conformity to Jesus according to the design of the Father is, *as St. Paul writes,* that He has predestined us *"to become conformed to the image of His Son, that He should be the firstborn among many brethren"* (Rm 8.29).

FROM CALVARY TO TABOR...

However, it is important to reflect well upon the fact that to arrive at such heights it is necessary to give complete sway to the Immaculate. She must become present and operative in all of the soul's faculties because it is there that She wishes to *transubstantiate* us into Herself. Hence, St. Maximilian asks these questions: *"Do you want Her to dwell permanently in your soul? Do you desire that She, and She alone, direct your thoughts and take possession of your entire heart? Do you desire to live totally for Her? If you truly want all of this, then open your whole heart before Her."*[236] Again, writing with ease: *"It is necessary that the external and internal tribulations, the*

---

[235] *De Nativitate B.M.V.,* sermo III.
[236] SK 1216

failures, listlessness, fatigue, derisions, setbacks, and other crosses purify and strengthen us."[237]

In following the school of St. Maximilian, it is both beautiful and important to note that he himself did not fail to turn to the Immaculate in times of active and passive purifications. *"I prayed to the Immaculate,"* he writes, *"that She might purify my thoughts, my words, and my actions from that which does not come from Her."*[238] The Saint specifies that *"as for me personally, the humiliations are indeed very necessary."*[239] He seems to be accusing himself when he writes, *"I do everything with much irritability. But with the help of the Immaculate I will correct myself."*[240] He reaches the point of lucidly outlining the path of these various purifications according to the plan of the Immaculate by recalling two significant mountains in the Bible: *"This is the tactic of the Immaculate: first Calvary, then Tabor."*[241]

St. Maximilian himself, therefore, exhorts us to comprehend the dynamic of the ascetical course made up more of challenges, difficulties, sacrifices, and bitterness than sweet consolations and caresses. *"We do not want to continually feel the sweetness of devotion to the Immaculate because this would be spiritual greed. Let us give Her permission to direct us as it pleases Her, and not how we ourselves want it. It is not always the time for sweet tenderness, even if this is very holy. Rather we need to be tried, treated harshly, abandoned and the like. Let us allow Her, therefore, the full freedom to utilize the means for our sanctification."*[242]

Thus, we too, with St. Maximilian, must be well aware of the fact that the active and passive purifications through the *Marian Vow* are a sure sign of advancing along the right path; it is the path of elevation by way of sufferings and crosses. *"He who labors for the Immaculate,"* the Saint writes, *"must suffer much. The Immaculate, too, suffered much. Besides, love lives and nourishes itself precisely with crosses."*[243]

As a result, the work of loving *transubstantiation* into the Immaculate so as to realize the perfect and supreme *christification* is exclusively bound up with that greater love which lives and increases amid sufferings. This greater love nourishes itself especially upon

---

[237] SK 56
[238] SK 308
[239] SK 361
[240] SK 991
[241] SK 383
[242] SK 504
[243] SK 402; cf. also SK 499

the Cross and there becomes a giant, as it were. *"My dear children, let us remember that love lives and is nourished by sacrifices. We thank the Immaculate for interior peace and for the ecstasy of love. Nonetheless, let us not forget that all of this, even if good and beautiful, is not the essence of love, and that love, or rather perfect love, can exist even without all of this."*[244]

It is fundamental that we comprehend this. St. Maximilian, as a matter of fact, explains this with great attention and insists that the true *"peak of love is the state in which Jesus found Himself upon the Cross when He said: 'My God, My God, why hast Thou forsaken Me?'"*[245] Therefore, the Saint is able to conclude with his usual concrete, practical suggestions: *"Without sacrifice there is no love: the sacrifice of the senses, above all of the eyes (particularly when one exits the friary and goes among seculars), the sacrifice of taste, of hearing and so on, but first and foremost, the sacrifice of the intellect and the will in holy obedience."*[246]

THE "HEART" OF SUFFERING

The Saint's discourse becomes evermore demanding and, in the end, his teaching does not spare any severe blow in the realm of self-denial. This self-renunciation is to be realized to such an extent and in such a manner as to be truly radical, so radical as to overturn even the very aversion to sacrifices by welcoming and even directly requesting them. St. Maximilian writes: *"When love for Her, for the goodness of God in Her, for that divine Heart which is personified in Her, when such love has grabbed hold of us and penetrated within, then sacrifices will become 'a necessity for the soul.'"* Consequently, *"the soul will desire to give constant and ever new and profound demonstrations of love, and such demonstrations are none other than 'sacrifices.'"*[247]

Further, it is important to reflect upon the fact that the mystical ascent of those who live out the *Marian Vow* must be modeled upon and take the form of the Immaculate Herself since they are to be *transubstantiated* into Her. If we who belong to the Immaculate know the "mysteries" of the Rosary (joyful, luminous, sorrowful, and glorious) which marked the entire path of Her earthly existence

---
[244] SK 503
[245] Ibid.
[246] Ibid.
[247] Ibid.

with Christ until She entered Paradise, then we know what must mark the mystical ascent of those who live the *Marian Vow* fully and faithfully. At this point we need to bring up the particular discussion about that truth of Faith (not yet defined) of the most crucial mystery of Mary Most Holy, namely the mystery of Her active and painful cooperation in the work of universal Redemption as the Mother *Coredemptrix*, indissolubly united in a subordinate manner to Her Son, the *Redeemer*.

The tormenting mystery of the *Coredemption* can and must be considered the *heart* of that ineffable mystery of Mary Most Holy who became our "Mother in the order of grace" on Calvary, as Vatican II says (LG 61), giving birth to us amid the sorrow and anguish of delivery (cf. Apoc 12:1).

According to the constant doctrine of the Church, we know that the *Coredemptrix* was concrucified with the Redeemer for us on the Cross. St. Pio of Pietrelcina states this with blinding clarity when he affirms that on Calvary *"Mary is crucified with Jesus. It is the martyrdom of the heart"*;[248] and it was a martyrdom of atrocious, unspeakable sufferings, as St. Pio further explains: *"The Madonna, like Jesus, suffered all of the pains of Hell on Calvary."*[249]

Well then, what must be the response on the part of Her children who have taken the *Marian Vow*? What level of participation is to be theirs? What measure of generosity should animate them as they stand close to Her at the foot of the Cross, or rather united with *"this our dear Coredemptrix"* as St. Pio calls Her?[250]

In a letter to Sr. Ermentrude of Bruges, St. Clare of Assisi solicitously recommends assiduous meditation upon Our Lady of Sorrows, the Coredemptrix, at Calvary: *"Meditate tirelessly upon the mystery of the Cross and the sorrows of the Mother who stood at the foot of the Cross."*[251]

---

[248] Cf. *Padre Pio parla della Madonna*, p.60.
[249] *Padre Pio parla della Madonna*, p.112.
[250] *Epistolario*, vol. I, p. 384.
[251] St. Clare, *Letters* (FF 2915).

St. Maximilian exhorts us to *"lay our very life before Her in sacrifice."*[252] This means generosity in making sacrifices and offering voluntary penances so as to bring about our conversion and cooperate in the conversion of others; this means self-denial through continual mortifications and renouncements because, as again St. Maximilian teaches using an excellent image: *"A sculptor will never succeed in transforming a block of stone into a statue with caresses alone, but must carve and chisel."*[253]

If we look at our models, in fact, we immediately see how they lovingly contemplated and participated in the mystery of Mary's Coredemption. They sought to share in the sufferings of Our Lady of Sorrows at the foot of the Cross through offering themselves as crucified victims with bloody stigmatization (St. Francis of Assisi and St. Pio of Pietrelcina); with twenty-eight years of sickness on an austere bed (St. Clare of Assisi); and with the cruel martyrdom in the starvation bunker of Auschwitz (St. Maximilian M. Kolbe).

TRIAL UPON TRIAL...

It is sufficient to read through the biographies of St. Francis, St. Clare, St. Maximilian, and St. Pio to discover the incredible abundance of trials and tribulations they had to undergo; the manner and measure of suffering they endured was, humanly speaking, incalculable. God only knows the sum total of the trials and tribulations that they suffered and offered with love as victims.

In St. Maximilian's life, for example, it can be said that the sum of his sacrifices and trials during his religious life and apostolic activity was proportionate to his exceptional sanctity and his colossal apostolic activity for the Immaculate. It is certainly no exaggeration for anyone who knows his life to say that trials never diminished nor knew of mitigation in his life. His life was characterized by suffering from youth with ailments and physical pains until his death through the glorious martyrdom in the most atrocious starvation bunker of Auschwitz. We only know a fraction of all the interior anguish, difficulties, and conflicts he endured throughout his life from his confreres and others outside the community. Then there were those

---

[252] SK 895
[253] SK 52

most lacerating interior assaults which were capable, at times, of leading him upon the brink of despair for his own salvation.

"*How many times,*" the Saint was able to write, "*I seem to have no faith, no hope, and not even to sense love. The devil insinuates the question: 'Why have you come here?' and my nature feels aversion to all the concerns, nuisances, and sufferings and would like an idle and slothful serenity.*"[254]

The Saint's words are realistic and incisive. In fact, he had to experience many dramas and tragedies and to undergo interior storms and exterior devastations in his life. In particular, he sacrificed himself without any reserve for the foundation of the two Cities of the Immaculate in Poland and Japan. He poured himself out and consumed himself for it all, even to the point of undergoing his ultimate and tremendous "holocaust" in the Hellish concentration and death camp—Auschwitz (*Oswiecim* in Polish). There his entire life of immolation was crowned by his voluntary, truly dreadful martyrdom in the lugubrious hunger bunker.

There is a phrase of his, however, which seems to be a battle cry or even a song of victory. This resounds from St. Maximilian's heart, from the heart of this new martyr of the twentieth century: "*The Immaculate leads us with a strong and loving hand accompanying us through the thorns, along the impassible paths, among the abysses, and in the midst of cyclones. The devil, for his part, is seeking to injure me in every way. We, however, seek to press evermore closely around Her and in this way we move forward, or rather we fly with great speed. Glory to Her for everything.*"[255]

Among all of these words of the Saint, the expression "*we fly with great speed*" is especially meaningful. This characteristic expression can call to mind the "*flight of the spirit*" in infused contemplation, or, even more so, the "*transforming love*" which is realized in the "*fire of love*" in one's heart (the *incendium amoris* of St. Bonaventure's "*The Triple Way*"), and which immerses the soul into that ineffable Trinitarian experience of the supreme, divine reality of the highest and most consummate mystical life.

> This image of "flight" which St. Maximilian makes use of is truly beautiful. With the Immaculate, therefore, closely pressed to Her, one flies "*with great speed*" towards the highest heavens. In all truth, a most intimate union with the

---

[254] SK 315; cf. also SK 347, 373
[255] SK 497

Immaculate is the most valuable and exquisite fruit of that purification which liberates one from all that is not of Her and which unites the soul to Her to the point of bringing about that mystical identification with Her called, by St. Maximilian, *transubstantiation* into Her.

It has rightly been said that "slowly but surely, souls, through Our Lady's continuous interventions, feel ever more emptied of that which is earthly through an ever more intense practice of negative asceticism. This asceticism is wholly characterized by a Marian spirit and these souls experience within themselves something which attracts them ever more and more to Mary, to the point of forming, in a certain sense, but one spirit with Her. To explain it with words already noted, they speak of transformation into and identification with the Virgin."[256]

CONTEMPLATIVE PRAYER

With regards to the contemplative life, it has to be pointed out that our seraphic religious life is and must be above all *contemplative*. Unfortunately, this is readily forgotten with a great deal of superficiality. Our seraphic form of the consecrated life is essentially *contemplative-active*. Therefore, it is first of all *contemplative*, and then *active*. But it is so easy to fall into thinking that the contemplative life is only that which is lived in cloistered monasteries, contemplative convents, hermitages, and the like. Consequently, in practice, the lion's share of our daily life comes to be occupied primarily by activities to accomplish, external duties to tend to, and the apostolate to sustain and increase more and more.

This unfortunately common error is fatal. It perverts the nature of our form of consecrated life by putting things upside down. Hence, that which is primary—*contemplation*—comes to be substituted by that which is secondary—*action*. And this alone explains the sterility of much of our religious life. If *contemplation* is, in fact, the *soul* of religious life, while *action* is the *body*, then it is obvious that the flowering and fruitfulness of religious life is linked first and foremost

---

[256] S. Ragazzini, *Maria vita dell'anima*, p. 319.

with the vitality of *contemplation*: if this fails, the entire religious life cannot help but fail with it.

It is our duty, therefore, not only to guard the *primacy* of the contemplative life, but even to cultivate it without omission or indolence: through silence, recollection, daily mental prayer (meditation), affective prayer, aspirations, and other advances towards infused contemplation.

It is this infused contemplation, therefore:

- which is, in reality, the supreme activity of the human spirit through the power of the Holy Spirit;

- which brings one to penetrate and be immersed in God who is *"intellectual Light full of love"*;[257]

- which is completely the *"science of love"* as St. John of the Cross calls it;[258]

- which brings one to know and taste *"the things that are above, where Christ is seated at the right hand of God"* (Col 3:1);

- which leads to the *transforming* and *consummating* union of love with God, as St. Bonaventure teaches when he says that "the affective power [in the sense of a capacity in the soul] unites more to that which is lovable than the cognitive does to that which is knowable, and thus love transforms the one loving into the beloved."[259]

Holy Mother St. Clare is a sublime master and model of contemplation. She synthesizes all things at the summit of union with God when she states with dazzling simplicity that we can come to be transformed *"entirely into the image of His divinity by means of contemplation."*[260]

In order to grasp how connatural the *Marian Vow* and the *contemplative* life are, it is enough to reflect on the fact that the *Marian Vow*, by its very nature, places us on that *"white ladder"* or,

---

[257] *Paradiso*, XXX, 40.
[258] *Dark Night*, II, 18, 5.
[259] *In III Sententiarum*, d. 6, art. 2, q. 1, ad 2.
[260] St. Clare, *Letters* (FF 2888).

adopting the happy expression of St. John Climacus, upon that most exalted *"heavenly ladder"* which is the Immaculate.

It is St. Maximilian himself who tells us that with unlimited consecration to the Immaculate, *"God has given us this white ladder and desires that we, ascending upon it, might come to Him, or rather that She, after having pressed us to Her motherly Heart, might bring us to God."*[261] What a tremendous and joyful grace this is! St. Maximilian is right, therefore, in telling all of us: *"The knowledge of belonging completely to the Immaculate fills us with boundless joy."*[262]

Without a doubt we can also consider the fact that the *Marian Vow* binds us incessantly to the contemplative life, to the highest and most divine contemplative life of the Immaculate Herself. Through contemplation She, in fact, wants to *transubstantiate* us into Herself, She who is the *"All-divinized Lady,"* as St. Peter Damian so beautifully and brilliantly calls Her. She is *"so united to God through love,"* writes St. Maximilian, *"that She is exalted above not only the Saints, but even the Angels, the Archangels, the Cherubim, the Seraphim…"*[263]

We, therefore, who strive faithfully to live the *Marian Vow* through a perfect observance of the *Book of Sanctification,* receive the gift to climb to these heights. We are given the opportunity to ascend the steps of the contemplative life through the *active and passive purifications* which occur through the life of prayer, penance, and mortification pushing us towards the *kenosis* (self-emptying) of ourselves and the "disappearance" of ourselves in the Immaculate. This is in perfect harmony with St. Maximilian's expressions. He explains this in precisely these terms: *"Let us disappear in Her! May She alone remain, and we in Her, a part of Her…"*;[264] and again: *"The essence […] is to annihilate oneself and to become Her."*[265]

When we reach this point, in fact, there takes place the most complete and perfect union of Christ within, that is the most exalted and authentic *christification* through the working of the Holy Spirit. This is because it is precisely in the Immaculate, and in Her alone, that this *christification* is brought about and, one could say, it is only *"natural."* As St. Maximilian puts it: *"In the womb of the Immaculate the soul is reborn in the form of Jesus Christ."*[266]

---

[261] SK 461
[262] SK 834
[263] SK 461
[264] Ibid.
[265] SK 579
[266] SK 1295

WITH HER, IN HER, BY HER...

Thus, St. Maximilian presents the divine ascent to the supreme life and experience of the inner life of the Trinity as having its starting point in the Immaculate, an ascent which then continues with the Immaculate who is ineffably one with the Holy Spirit and indissolubly united with Him as His Spouse. The Saint tells us that it is indeed in and with the Immaculate that the soul is lifted up *"as with wings of God's love that carry it where the Holy Spirit breathes, shattering every barrier."*[267]

It is with and in the Immaculate, therefore, that the mystical ascent to the Trinitarian life and the experience of the indwelling Trinity takes place. Why? Because, as St. Maximilian once again writes, *"We serve Jesus with, in, and by means of Her; and with and by means of Him, God the Father. And the Holy Spirit? He is within the Immaculate [...] and this union is so ineffable and perfect that the Holy Spirit acts solely by means of the Father and the Immaculate, His Spouse."*[268]

Hence, the journey of the soul is well-defined in the mind and words of St. Maximilian: the mystical ascent into the bosom of the Father occurs only along this road, *"namely by means of the Holy Spirit and the Son, in other words through the Immaculate, the Spouse of the Holy Spirit."*[269]

St. Maximilian's thought is plainly manifest regarding the unity of action between the Holy Spirit and the Immaculate, His Spouse. He notes that the Holy Spirit works solely *"with Mary, in Mary and by means of Mary."*[270] It follows that even if the Holy Spirit seems not to be named and therefore not to be present and working, He is nonetheless always present and working *in the Immaculate* and *by means of the Immaculate* who is His indissoluble, ever-virgin Bride.

As a result of this meditation upon the spousal, indissoluble unity between the Holy Spirit and the Immaculate Virgin, St. Maximilian is able to write: *"In reality, therefore, we are entirely, completely, and exclusively consecrated to the Immaculate with all of our actions; and in Her and by means of Her we are consecrated always entirely, completely, and exclusively to Jesus Christ; in Him, then, and by*

---

[267] SK 1301
[268] SK 634
[269] SK 643
[270] SK 1229; cf. also SK 1286.

means of Him, we are consecrated entirely, completely, and exclusively to our heavenly Father."[271]

This is how the divine ascent takes place through that journey which elevates the soul and immerses it in the bosom of the Father. It seems clear, therefore, that we *"will never succeed in doing this without the Son and without our Mother."*[272] Rather, it is precisely the Virgin Mother, with and under the action of the Holy Spirit, who will bring this divine ascent to completion. St. Maximilian insists upon saying that *"She alone must instruct each of us in every instant; She must direct us, transform us into Herself, in such wise that it is no longer we who live, but She in us, just as Jesus lives in Her, and the Father in the Son."*[273]

IN THE IMMACULATE WITH THE HOLY SPIRIT

The Immaculate is in us with Her indissoluble spousal union with the Holy Spirit, while the Word Incarnate is in the Immaculate, and the eternal Father is in the Son. This is the connatural connection which forms the essence of the divine ascent to transforming union in the experience of the Trinity within.[274] This is St. Maximilian's teaching which is validated by his personal experience, especially in the last years of his life and concluded by martyrdom in the hellish death camp of Auschwitz.

Pointing out once again the task of the Immaculate in our sanctification, St. Maximilian explains that Jesus is *"the fruit of the love of God, One and Three, for Mary Immaculate"*; everyone else is called to become a child of God and brother of Christ in the same way, namely by means of Mary in union with the Holy Spirit. There is no other way for us to attain our divine sonship; this is the divine design of the Incarnation.

"Therefore," the Saint writes, *"he who does not wish to have Mary Immaculate for Mother will not have Christ for his brother, neither will God the Father send him the Son, nor will the Son descend into his soul, nor will the Holy Spirit with His own graces form the Mystical Body upon the model of Christ, because all of this happens in Mary Immaculate, full of grace, and solely in Mary."*[275]

---

[271] SK 643
[272] Ibid.
[273] SK 556
[274] *sperienza intratrinitaria* in Italian rendered here as the "experience of the inner life of the Trinity."
[275] SK 1295, 1296

CHAPTER 11
THE MARIAN VOW AND THE PRIESTHOOD

For all of the Franciscans of the Immaculate who have the divine call and gift of the ministerial priesthood, they well understand that living the *Marian Vow* faithfully, and not in mediocrity, constitutes the best guarantee of their personal holiness and of the pastoral fruitfulness of the priesthood itself for the good of the People of God.

What Padre Pio of Pietrelcina said one day to a young Capuchin priest holds true today and always: *"Only through associating the Madonna with your priesthood will you become efficacious in the field of grace so as to make bud forth children of God and saints in this world."*[276]

It does not take much reflection, in fact, to immediately discover that there is a basic and spontaneous affinity between the sacramental priesthood and the *Marian Vow*. From this can be seen that natural dynamic of grace existing between the *priesthood* and the *Marian Vow*. The symbiosis and synergy of divine grace makes them present to one another on a *natural level*, once could say, in the exercise of the ministerial priesthood by one consecrated without limits to the Immaculate with the *Marian Vow*.

"PERSONIFYING" JESUS THE PRIEST

As we know, the priest is an *alter Christus* in the fullest and most authentic way insofar as it can be said that he *"personifies"* Jesus and is *"personified"* by Christ the Priest.[277] With some reflection, we quickly realize that if the priest comes to "personify" Jesus, then this means that he is a son of Mary in an entirely special way. He

---

[276] Cf. *Padre Pio parla della Madonna*, p. 45.
[277] The Italian verb here, *impersonare*, readily connotes the doctrine that the priest stands *in persona Christi* according to the Latin expression.

therefore belongs to Her in a unique and singular manner since to be "personified" by Jesus means to realize the most true *conformity* to Jesus, the *"Firstborn"* (Rm 8:29).

Since the priest who has taken the *Marian Vow* is the "absolute property" of the Immaculate, it follows that the *Marian Vow* radicalizes to the utmost his belonging to Her specifically as a *priest*. Hence, he must be dedicated in a singular way to live out this filial, unlimited belonging to Her as one, who more than any other, "personifies" Her divine Son, "personifies" Jesus the Priest, "personifies" Jesus *the High Priest* with the divine mission and primary responsibility of being "Head" and "Teacher" of the People of God entrusted to his care.

It is well understood, therefore, how important and necessary it is for the priest, more so than any other Christian, to enter a complete and constant identification of love with Jesus. We are speaking here of a *personalized* identification which is unique, indelible, and fixed in time and space by an eternal, sacramental character: *"You are a priest forever!"*

As we all know, the priest must "personify" Jesus not just when he celebrates at the altar or remits sins when confessing, nor simply when preaching or baptizing or administering the anointing of the sick, but rather he must personify Him always and everywhere. This personification of Christ must continue in every moment of the day. It does not admit of divisions, dissociations, or suspensions of any sort, but requires that the whole day be thoroughly priestly in nature.

If the *Marian Vow* faithfully lived out brings us to the highest "conformity" to Jesus within the Immaculate's "womb," then it must be said that this applies all the more to the Franciscan priest of the Immaculate. In living the *Marian Vow* he can have, more so than anyone else, that "face which most resembles Christ";[278] and he can have this always and everywhere, especially at the altar, in the confessional, at the pulpit, and in the exercise of his ministerial priesthood. His full *conformity-to-Mary* is also his most complete and priestly *conformity-to-Christ*.

"GRACE UPON GRACE"

Besides, if the priesthood is an exceptional grace, it is also true that it involves a need for the priest to receive many graces in order

---
[278] *Paradiso*, XXXII, 85–86.

to bear the weight of the great responsibility he has and to carry out in a holy, fruitful manner the sublime mission which has been entrusted to him for the sake of all mankind [in Latin *"pro hominibus constituitur"*] (Heb 5:1).

To be the "absolute property" of the Immaculate by way of the *Marian Vow* means just that: he can draw forth every grace in abundance from the Heart of the Immaculate Mediatrix of all graces; furthermore, he should be governed by the *Mother of Divine Grace* in everything and for everything. In this way, his priesthood will be a constant radiation and expansion of graces; it will be fruitful, in spite of the many dangers in the world, and will bring forth salvation and every possible blessing for both the priest himself as well as for all of the souls entrusted to his pastoral care.

If the Immaculate is the *Treasurer of all graces,* then it can readily be deduced how the priest, in the measure that he is faithful to the *Marian Vow,* (which makes him the Immaculate's "absolute property,") will in that measure be all the more capable of being filled with "grace upon grace" through Her and obtain from Her abundant graces which will produce much fruit in the ministry he has to accomplish. This is how the fruits of the apostolate are to be understood for the conversion of souls and their being led into the sheepfold, led and even carried to eternal salvation and holiness. It is above all through living out the *Marian Vow* to the point of being transubstantiated into the Immaculate that the priest becomes a faithful minister of the Gospel and *"steward of the mysteries of God"* (1 Cor 4:1; cf. 2 Cor 6:4).

The example of St. Maximilian M. Kolbe is, in this regard, certainly one of the most eloquent and astonishing. His priesthood was totally Marian; his apostolic endeavors were tireless and fruitful in all fields; in the end he was transfigured in a martyrdom of charity which he faced with *"my Immaculate and my all"* in the death camp of Auschwitz. "In celebrating Holy Mass, Fr. Maximilian always had a radiant face": this was the magnificent eye-witness testimony of one of the friars, and there were many others recorded as well.[279]

And what of St. Pio of Pietrelcina? He could sincerely say, *"In my priestly action I have had one exemplar, one point of reference: the Madonna."*[280] When he observed the extraordinary fruits of grace from the maternal presence and assistance of Our Lady in his

---

[279] Cf. G. Lentini, *Massimiliano Kolbe*, p. 203.
[280] Cf. *Padre Pio parla della Madonna*, p. 207.

ministerial priesthood, Padre Pio commented: *"I have the impression that She is doing everything in my stead."*[281]

From these and many other examples of Saints who were priests particularly bound to Our Lady, it is understood that the Mother and Mediatrix of all graces is all the more committed to being near Her beloved priests in order to make their ministry of the altar and of reconciliation rich in blessings.

ENAMORED OF JESUS

Moreover, the priest must be enamored of Jesus even to the fullness of the transforming and consummating union of love. Who, then, will obtain this sublime love and how could anyone love Jesus more perfectly than by living out the *Marian Vow*? Living the *Marian Vow* actually means identifying oneself, "losing oneself" in the Immaculate in order to love Jesus with the very Heart of the Immaculate and simultaneously allowing Jesus to love Her with our heart. With what heart shall the Immaculate love Jesus more willingly than the consecrated heart of a priest who faithfully belongs to Her as Her "absolute property?"

It is evident, however, that the priest's loving response has to be entirely personal and free. Love cannot be imposed because it is born from within, it blossoms from the interior of the heart and is but one with the heart. First and foremost, therefore, it is necessary to *choose* to love Jesus, and therefore to nourish the commitment and effort to love Him by cultivating and multiplying the movements of the will, the impulses of the heart, and the strains of the spirit through an ever more passionate and ardent longing directed towards Him. If the ancient saying is true that *"one learns to love by loving,"* then clearly love grows only by the constant renewal and increase of acts of love which make up and express that which is specifically called *"being in love."*

He who passionately lives the *Marian Vow*, cannot help but be made a sharer in the *Immaculate's love for Jesus*. Moreover, he is able to aspire to this in the most complete and perfect measure possible, namely to be urged on even to a full *absorption* and *fusion* of his heart with the very Heart of the Immaculate, if we can speak in such fashion.

---

[281] *Padre Pio parla della Madonna*, p. 212.

The Immaculate, for Her part, is She who in the Holy Spirit so fully united Her Heart with Christ's so as to really form *"but one Heart"* with Him, as St. John Eudes so brilliantly taught. It is known that this Saint loved to speak and write at length specifically about the fusion of the Hearts of Jesus and Mary, so much so that, for him, in reality, Jesus and Mary do not have two Hearts, but one *"single"* Heart.

What this means, then, is that the heart of the priest living out the *Marian Vow* becomes united with the Heart of the Immaculate which is one with the divine Heart of Jesus. In this way, all three of these hearts truly come to form but *"one single Heart."* Thus, we could speak of a "loving trinity in one single Heart" that is in that unique Love which is the Holy Spirit. What a mystery of divine love!

A BUILDER OF THE CHURCH

The priest is pledged to work for the edification of Christ's Mystical Body which is the Church (cf. Eph 4:12). He must love the Church, therefore, as the Body of Christ who is its Head. The Body is made up of many members, namely all the souls in need of salvation and sanctification. Love the Church; live the Church; be the Church! The priest is the first called to this, and he is called personally.

Well then, the Franciscan priest of the Immaculate who lives out the *Marian Vow* will, as he himself is marianized and transfigured into the Immaculate, gradually come to find himself entirely in She who is the *"Virgin made Church,"* according to the splendid expression of our Seraphic Father St. Francis.[282] In other words, he too "becomes the Church" with She who so profoundly "personifies" the Church, who is the "most loving Mother" (LG 53) of the entire Church and of the "pastors and faithful," as Pope Paul VI states.

St. Maximilian was a priest, martyr, and tireless apostle who himself "became the Church." This is seen in his construction of the Cities of the Immaculate, both of which could be likened to the *"city set on a mountain"* mentioned in the Gospel (Mt 5:14). His ardent zeal sought to convert and save all souls *"through the Immaculate"* with missionary plans intended to conquer and expand from one continent to another throughout the world; he desired that all humanity might be incorporated into the one Church, which is

---

[282] *Salutation of the Blessed Virgin* (FF 259)

the Mystical Body of Christ, and of which the Immaculate is the Mother and Mediatrix.

St. Pio of Pietrelcina was a Franciscan priest who bore the stigmata. He was a man of prayer who shed his very blood while consuming himself for fifty years in administering sacramental Confession, a ministry which he accomplished entirely under the gaze of the *Madonna delle Grazie* in the Marian Shrine of San Giovanni Rotondo. In this way he edified the Church with that extraordinary *"worldwide clientele"* of all of his spiritual children, as Pope Paul VI put it, who gathered together and organized *"prayer groups"* which are present and active throughout the world.

These are two priests who built up the Church in union with the Immaculate, the "Mother of the Church." Theirs was a fervent love, the type of love *"which directs us,"* says St. Maximilian, *"towards the conquest of all hearts which are living at present and shall live in the future, and this as quickly as possible, as quickly as possible, as quickly as possible."*[283] This must be the fervent and vigilant longing of every true and operative priest in the Franciscans of the Immaculate who desires to live faithfully and intensely his *Marian Vow*.

THE FATHER OF SOULS

What is more, the priest must draw near to souls, touch hearts, enlighten minds, and bend obstinate wills in order to convert and save the souls entrusted to him. These are all very delicate operations of grace, to be sure. However, the priest with the *Marian Vow* will have grace upon grace for every soul; he will know how to touch hearts with the maternal delicateness of the Immaculate. Why? Because he is docilely living and working by means of the Immaculate.

The maternal presence of the Immaculate cannot but inspire in "Her" priest the most generous, warm, attentive, caring, enlightening, and operative sentiments, as is evident from the admirable life of St. Maximilian. It can be said without a doubt that priestly fatherhood is the closest thing to Mary's motherhood and maternal mediation. Hence, it is also the closest in efficaciously "mediating" graces for souls: graces of conversion, salvation, spiritual growth, and sanctification.

The priest who is living his *Marian Vow* knows well how to be a docile instrument in the hands of the Immaculate; he is aware

---
[283] SK 1325

that *"She distributes all the graces of conversion and sanctification to the inhabitants of this valley of tears."* He is also aware that he needs to ask all graces of Her for the salvation and sanctification of the souls entrusted to him; he must pray to the Immaculate with confidence *"because,"* as St. Maximilian once wrote to Her, *"every grace that streams forth from the most sweet Heart of Jesus comes to us through Your hands."*[284]

No one more than a priest living the *Marian Vow* can experience that love which ignites and, as St. Maximilian says, *"cannot find its place in the limits of the heart, but spreads out like wildfire and inflames, devours, and absorbs other hearts."*[285] It must be pondered and understood, therefore, that the *Marian Vow* pushes priestly fatherhood to the maximum quotient of love for giving, saving, and sanctifying the life of souls through that love which *"spreads like wildfire, inflames, devours, and absorbs other hearts."*

If St. Maximilian holds that *"love knows no limits,"* then this must be true in a particular way for the priest who is fully living out the *Marian Vow*. Clearly this "unlimited" love cannot help but be total, courageous, heroic, and sacrificial.[286] It is very significant to note that St. Maximilian, in one of his lists where he had written the phrase *"love knows no limits,"* traced a little cross above the word *"love"* in red ink:[287] it was a sign of that love unto the shedding of *blood* which crimsoned St. Maximilian's whole life with his recurring hemoptysis and his painful death as a martyr.

IN THE HOUR OF TRIAL

Bitter days will come in the life of a priest. There will be falls, mistakes, failures, storms of every sort, internal and external sufferings, moral anguish, and physical pain. It must be emphasized, therefore, that when these days come, the *Marian Vow* will offer him the most solid and efficacious support, especially when the Vow is

---

[284] SK 1029
[285] SK 1325
[286] *martiriale* in Italian, translated here as "sacrificial."
[287] SK 968

accompanied with *spiritual direction*—precious above all when the soul is going through trials. The priest who has taken the *Marian Vow* is the Immaculate's "absolute property" and can always and even must, trust in Her. The Immaculate will take care of him. She will help him to rise from his falls. She will assist him in fruitfully enduring every trial. This is because in taking the *Marian Vow* he offered himself to the Immaculate without limits and thus disposed himself for every sacrifice, even to becoming a martyr and victim of love for the salvation of souls.

In this, too, the example and teaching of St. Maximilian were amazing. *"In the event of a fall,"* the Saint teaches, *"offer yourself immediately to Her, together with the entire matter of your fall, and ask for forgiveness: 'My dear Mother, forgive me and beseech for forgiveness from Jesus for me.'"*[288] Again, regarding falls, the Saint writes in a telegraph: *"After a fall run quickly to Mary Immaculate."*[289]

One personal example of a fall in the Saint's life is contained in one of his letters to his brother: *"In writing letters in Japanese I caved in to a thought of pride, namely that in some way I was managing to express myself in this language. But I immediately felt that my bond of love with the Immaculate had become cold. I was seated before the little statue of Her and it seemed as if She wanted to reproach me, that She was angry!"* He continues by suggesting that in order to conquer any moment of weakness we should offer our fault to the Immaculate *"by merely pronouncing the name of 'Mary,' just as* I did a moment ago." He then recommends engaging in "giving pleasure to Her with *the next immediate action, as I am doing in this very moment."*[290]

We all know that the battle against our personal defects can be distressing; it can wear us out and be unnerving. With the weight of responsibilities and tribulations that every priest has, frequently discouragement can set in and, more than anything else, can cause the priest to break down. What to do? For a priest of the Franciscans of the Immaculate, the response is bound up with the vitality of the *Marian Vow*.

> Because of the special presence of the Immaculate who is close to the priest who is Her "property," the thought of St. Maximilian can be readily understood. He wrote to himself once during his personal meditation: *"With the help of the*

---

[288] SK 1334
[289] SK 965
[290] SK 504

Immaculate you will conquer yourself and contribute greatly to the salvation of souls. Let yourself be led by Her immaculate little hands; be Her instrument; up to now no one has had recourse to Her in vain. Entrust all of your undertakings to Her and She will deign to take care of them. In Her immaculate little hands victory is certain."[291] And elsewhere we find words from the Saint that are very encouraging for any priest experiencing his own inadequacies and failures: *"Within the little hands of the Immaculate, you can do everything. Entrust to Her everything that you do not know or are not capable of doing, and then you shall know and succeed in doing that which will give the greatest glory possible to God, without limits. She does not refuse anything to sinners, while the most Sacred Heart of Jesus does not know how to refuse anything to Her."*[292]

It is written of St. Pio, as well, that in times of difficulty and trouble he "resolved everything through the Madonna," our heavenly Mother and Advocate of grace. In these moments he turned to Her continually and would frequently go to Confession, confessing even daily during certain periods. Nearness to Her is what guaranteed every true fruit of the ministerial priesthood. Thus, he was able to say: *"If I did not always sense the most holy Virgin at my side, intent upon dispensing graces in abundance, then I would not consider myself a poor philanthropist, but rather I would be a 'poor man.'"*[293]

A TOTALLY MARIAN PRIEST

It goes without saying that the Franciscan priest of the Immaculate, by virtue of the *Marian Vow*, must be "Marian" *par excellence*. He must be a priest who not only prays much to the Immaculate, but who loves Her immensely, who makes use of every means and occasion to make Her loved, who is always solicitous in using up all of his time for Her, and who tirelessly spends himself for Her so as to accomplish all by means of Her.

The *Marian Vow*, therefore, lived out faithfully, cannot help but transform a priest into an ardent, indefatigable apostle of prayer and

---
[291] SK 987 D
[292] SK 987 D 31S
[293] Cf. *Padre Pio parla della Madonna*, p. 212–213.

sacrifice, like St. Maximilian, who wanted to lead the whole world to Mary's feet. He strived in every way possible to contribute to the maximum exaltation of the Immaculate; he incessantly aspired from the depths of his heart to be able to give such a glory to the Immaculate as had never been given to Her by anyone else up to that time. In an act of consecration to the Immaculate he himself once wrote: *"Grant that I might lead the entire world to You. Grant that I might contribute to Your ever greater exaltation, to Your greatest possible exaltation. Grant that I might give You such glory that no one up to now has ever offered You."*[294]

This is what the *Marian Vow* is when fully active in the heart and apostolate of the Franciscan priest of the Immaculate. As a result, he becomes a powerful magnet attracting many souls to the Immaculate so that by means of Her they might swiftly and happily come to the Heart of Jesus, the Savior of mankind.

Then there is that beautiful image spoken by St. Pio regarding Our Lady's presence in all his priestly activity and ministry; he, in fact, wanted to be spiritually directed and assured by Her in everything. He would say: *"I feel myself to be a sailboat, moved by the breath of the Heavenly Mother. Even if lost in deep waters, I feel at peace. I am unable to say how I begin or finish my various undertakings; yet I do not feel uncertain because I am spiritually directed by Her."*[295]

What a treasure of grace and assurance of success when a priest is humble and generous in the hands of the divine Mother!

---

[294] SK 1305
[295] Cf. *Padre Pio parla della Madonna*, pp. 210–211.

CHAPTER 12
THE MARIAN VOW AND THE DEVOTIONAL LIFE OF THE FRANCISCANS OF THE IMMACULATE

Perhaps it would be useful at this point to draw out a few points of reference regarding the "Marian character" of the devotional life of every Franciscan of the Immaculate: priest, religious, and all those who have taken the *Marian Vow*. We will treat of simple, essential reference points which are concrete and practical, based primarily upon the life, example, and teachings of our special teachers and models, namely the four Patron Saints of our Institute: our Seraphic Father St. Francis, our Holy Mother St. Clare, St. Maximilian M. Kolbe, and St. Pio of Pietrelcina.

LITURGICAL PRAYER

The behavior and work which must accompany the active nature of the *Marian Vow* are first and foremost linked with the intensity of the life of *prayer* which must daily occupy the first place and must be exemplary and fervent in its expression. It is a fundamental and vital duty, therefore, to love prayer, to live prayer, and to seek to pray constantly as Our Lord commands: *"always pray"* (in Latin *oportet semper orare* Lk 18:1), and as our Seraphic Father St. Francis recommends: *"Pray always with a pure heart"* (*Rule*, Ch. 10).

Obviously, liturgical prayer always takes the first place both in terms of respect and value: the Holy Mass, the Liturgy of the Hours, and the Eucharistic Liturgy (Benediction and Adoration). Besides, we must keep in mind that liturgical prayer is the prayer of the Church, the prayer of the entire Mystical Body of Christ.

Let us remember the teaching of St. Maximilian who wrote in his personal notes: *"The Divine Office and the Holy Mass, celebrated well, renew an entire Diocese*";[296] and elsewhere he specifically insists upon love for the Liturgy of the Hours: *"By reciting well your prayers (the Divine Office), you are giving glory to God and obtaining many graces for Holy Church, for others, for your apostolate, and for yourself. How many conversions! Yet what a responsibility for negligence!"*[297]

Bl. Thomas of Celano writes the following of our Seraphic Father St. Francis: *"He recited the canonical Hours with reverence on a par with devotion [...] he always fulfilled his obligation of the Hours standing, without the hood, without looking around, and without interruption."*[298] Do we not have a lot learn?

CONTEMPLATIVE PRAYER

The *contemplative* life—which must have *primacy* of place in our form of religious life—cannot have real consistency without the support of daily contemplative prayer. If the prayer of a Franciscan, according to the *Seraphic Rule,* must reach the point of being continuous, as our Seraphic Father wished (in Latin *"orare semper ad Deum puro corde"* Rule, Ch. 10), how much more the prayer of those who have taken the *Marian Vow!* They must be all the more faithful to this continuous prayer according to the school of She who at least twice is carefully presented in the Gospel as being intimately recollected in meditation of the heart: *"Mary kept in mind all these things, pondering them in her heart"* (Lk 2:19, 51).

Concretely, our contemplative prayer must daily take substance primarily through communal and private meditation. This is to be cultivated with punctuality and accuracy in order that it may gradually become a necessity of the life of the spirit and an ardent passion of the heart which desires to increase more and more, blossoming into that contemplative, adoring love which *"transforms the lover into the Beloved,"* as St. Bonaventure puts it.

Besides, when lived out fully and faithfully, the *Marian Vow* genuinely carries within itself the mystical need for the highest and most fruitful contemplative love. It is the selfsame love that was found in our Seraphic Father St. Francis and our Holy Mother St. Clare, and is capable of leading us to *transubstantiation* into the

---

[296] SK 968
[297] SK 987 H
[298] Celano, *Second Life of St. Francis* (FF 683).

Immaculate in order to bring about the most complete and perfect *christification*.

The contemplative life, however, requires that our *"incessant"* prayer (cf. I Thes 5:17) be complemented with the aid that comes from our generous effort to practice silence, recollection, solitude, discretion, mortification of the senses, and detachment from anything that might impede complete union with the Immaculate.

Above all, growth in the life of contemplation requires and brings about a gradual passage from *mental* prayer to *affective* and therefore *contemplative* prayer in order to arrive at that direct communion with the Immaculate. This communion with Her is cultivated through our frequent thought and recourse to Her, through our renewed prayers and self-offerings to Her, and through our acts of love and filial conversations with Her who is our ever-vigilant Mother and is always "present" in a particular way to those consecrated to Her through the *Marian Vow*.

St. Pio of Pietrelcina teaches us to pray with profound recollection by keeping our eyes within the eyes of Our Lady. He expresses this as follows: *"As for prayer, as I have sought to keep my eyes within the eyes of our Heavenly Mother, so would I like it to be for my spiritual children."*[299]

THE CELEBRATION OF THE EUCHARIST

For the priest, the Eucharist in particular must be celebrated with the most intimate union between his soul and the Immaculate. Celebrating Holy Mass with the Immaculate within his soul! Will it not perhaps be Mary participating in the mystery of the Passion and Death of Jesus within the soul of "Her" priest and this in the most ineffable, sublime way possible? May the "sword" that pierced the Heart of the Crucified and the soul of the Coredemptrix at the foot of the Cross also pierce through the soul of the priest concrucified with Christ on the altar!

St. Maximilian celebrated Holy Mass with such recollection and devotion that the faithful could readily sense the mysterious reflection of a special presence of the Immaculate in him. She wrapped him in Her mantle and dwelt so thoroughly within him as to make even his face totally suffused with grace. St. Pio, on the other hand, with great simplicity once confided: *"Our Lady accompanies me*

---

[299] Cf. *Padre Pio parla della Madonna*, p. 207.

every morning at the altar along with our Seraphic Father St. Francis at the celebration of Holy Mass." If anyone, in fact, asked him if She were present at his celebration of the Mass, he would respond: *"And don't you see the Madonna at the altar during Mass?"*

All of us who have taken the *Marian Vow* must learn to appreciate each day the value of this privileged hour. We must immerse ourselves completely in the Immaculate in order to live the mystery of Calvary at the supreme level of a loving and sorrowful participation; this was precisely the living participation of the Immaculate Coredemptrix.

COMMUNION WITH THE IMMACULATE

Receiving Communion daily in union with the Immaculate has to be yet another constant commitment for those who have made the *Marian Vow*. St. Maximilian teaches with clarity: *"There is no better preparation for Holy Communion than to offer it totally to the Immaculate […] She will prepare our heart in the best of ways and we can thus be certain to procure the greatest joy and to manifest the greatest love for Jesus."*[300]

Again, with even more fervor, he writes: *"Receive Jesus in Holy Communion and accept everything from His hands with the humble disposition which the most holy Virgin Mary had at the moment of the Annunciation: 'Behold the handmaid of the Lord; be it done to me according to thy word'* (Lk 1:38)."[301] Elsewhere he writes: *"After Holy Communion, we will pray afresh to the Immaculate that She may welcome Jesus into our souls and make Him happy as no one else has ever succeeded in doing up to now."*[302]

Regarding this solicitous care in receiving the Eucharist, the Saint made this resolution: "Half of the day *in preparation,* half of the day *in thanksgiving; preparation and thanksgiving consist in* accomplishing well one's duties."[303]

The loving dedication of those who have taken the *Marian Vow* should be no less with regard to *spiritual communions* made frequently throughout the whole day. St. Maximilian once wrote this concise proposal in a list of spiritual resolutions: *"More frequent spiritual communions, at least every fifteen minutes."*[304] On a very encouraging

---
[300] SK 643
[301] SK 987 E
[302] SK 1234
[303] SK 962
[304] SK 987 I

note he attentively recalls that *"sometimes a* spiritual *communion contains within itself* the same graces *of a sacramental one."*[305]

VISITS TO THE BLESSED SACRAMENT

We are all acquainted with the fact that the life of St. Francis of Assisi was filled with frequent visits to the Blessed Sacrament—the number of hours and even whole nights he spent in Eucharistic Adoration is incalculable. St. Bonaventure writes that St. Francis used to flee from noise and the presence of persons who were distracting him from prayer and therefore "would seek out solitary places and go into solitude and into abandoned Churches to pray by night."[306]

Of St. Clare of Assisi, often depicted as holding a Eucharistic Ciborium just above her heart, we read in the *Omnibus* of Franciscan Sources that she would stay in the choir "in the evening after Compline, remaining for a long period in prayer with an abundance of tears. Around midnight she likewise would rise for prayer, when she was healthy, and would wake up the Sisters, touching them in silence."[307] In the *Legend of St. Clare* written by Bl. Thomas of Celano, it is written that the Saint "very frequently prostrated in prayer with her face to the ground, would bathe the soil with tears and gently kiss it: in such wise that she seemed to always have Jesus in her arms, whose feet she flooded with tears and imprinted with kisses."[308]

Fr. Pal, a companion of St. Maximilian during his formation, informs us that "love of Jesus in the Blessed Sacrament and of Our Lady touched his pious heart in every fiber of his being." Each day, the usual stops during his walk through Rome were "the Churches where the Blessed Sacrament was exposed."[309] We can also say he left us a precious inheritance of the *"ten Eucharistic visits"* which he sought to make by day or night from the time he was a young seminarian and of *perpetual* Eucharistic Adoration which he started in the Cities of the Immaculate both in Poland and Japan and was rewarded by the rapid increase in the number of vocations guaranteeing the continuity of hours of Adoration.

In conclusion, St. Pio was seen by endless crowds, yet he would pass many hours in prayer every day (not to mention the hours of

---

[305] SK 968
[306] Bonaventure, *Legenda Maior* (FF 1179).
[307] (St. Clare) *Process of Canonization* (FF 3071).
[308] Celano, *Legend of St. Clare* (FF 3197).
[309] G. Lentini, *Massimiliano Kolbe*, pp. 41–42.

prayer during the night!). He was accustomed to praying in the choir of the Church or in the nave off to the side of the sanctuary in the larger Church where he could see the Eucharistic Tabernacle and remain under the gaze of the *Madonna delle Grazie* at San Giovanni Rotondo. He would say to his spiritual children: *"If you want to find me, go near the Tabernacle!"*

SACRAMENTAL CONFESSION

It is necessary to give equal attention to frequent sacramental Confession (at least every week), making every effort to attentively preserve "*the immaculate* purity of conscience," as St. Maximilian puts it, "*and if it has come to be stained, let us seek to purify it as quickly as possible.*"[310]

We recall, in this regard, our Seraphic Father St. Francis. He usually confessed three times a week and every evening he would make his examination of conscience at the feet of Our Lady like a little child who humbly reveals to his mother his "little pranks" in order to be forgiven and purified by Her.

During certain periods of his life St. Pio went to Confession daily. A confrere once exhorted him not to be like a little baby who, as soon as he dirties a finger runs to his mother to make her clean it up; the Saint's response was: "That is what I do and that is what I want to do. You are better than me: you know how to purify yourself and make less use of the confessor. With the help of God I hope to never reach the point of believing myself to be self-sufficient."

It can be said that the *Marian Vow* is also the equivalent to a vow of *immaculateness*: this *immaculateness* is specifically acquired through frequent, well-made sacramental *Confession*, accompanied by sorrow and love.

> And it is important to recall the great value of *spiritual direction*—if possible, always under a priest of the Franciscans of the Immaculate. This is of primary importance if we want to guarantee ongoing growth in our spiritual life and the possibility of reaching perfect *conformity to Jesus in the Heart of the Immaculate* in accord with the *Marian Vow*.

---

[310] SK 892

From spiritual theology we can readily comprehend that it is practically impossible, in effect, to think we are seriously committed to advancing in the spiritual life without constant and accurate *spiritual direction*—preferably with a priest who is faithfully living the *Marian Vow*.

CONTINUAL MARIAN PRAYER

As we know, the *Marian Vow* carries within itself the grace of constant union with the Immaculate. Hence, our life cannot be other than a life of *continual prayer,* that is to say, a life of uninterrupted communion of prayer between the Immaculate and our soul.

Those who have taken the *Marian Vow* should live out to the letter the practical recommendation of St. Maximilian: *"Linger often with the Immaculate, converse frequently with Her, frequently pause and speak familiarly with Her, and you shall become ever more like Her."*[311]

Looking to St. Maximilian's marvelous example, we too should live constantly with the Immaculate as the *"fixed idea"* of our minds, the *"mad love"* burning in our hearts, and the *"feverish action"* coming from our wills.

According to St. Maximilian, frequent and quick prayers must be offered *"before work: 'Mary' (in order to accomplish it with love)."*[312] Or again: *"Before every action, after them, and in the middle of difficulties: 'Mary,' so that She might deign to take possession of it and do with it as She pleases."*[313] Once again: *"Mary, Mary, Mary: this is your life, before every activity, in the midst of difficulties, and at the end [of every action]."*[314]

Following the lead of St. Maximilian we must always cultivate the so-called "small change" prayers which are the *Marian ejaculations* (recalling especially this one: *"Sweet Heart of Mary, make me love you like crazy!"*[315]). We must also foster those *glances* towards Our Lady's images, wherever we may encounter them. Finally, we ought

---

[311] SK 1367
[312] SK 964
[313] SK 974
[314] SK 980
[315] In Italian: *"Dolce Cuore di Maria, fa ch'io t'ami alla follia!"* A more literal translation would read "Sweet Heart of Mary, make me love you unto foolishness/madness/lunacy" or "…bring it about that I may love you unto…"; these more literal translations completely lose the rhyme and meter of the Italian original; hence the compromised version cited above.

to cultivate the prayer of frequent *kisses* offered to our Immaculate Mother in our heart by kissing the Miraculous Medal which we carry over our heart.

Regarding ongoing Marian prayer, we have only to call to mind and imitate our Seraphic Father St. Francis. Bl. Thomas of Celano describes him as follows: *"He surrounded the Mother of Jesus with unspeakable love […]. In Her honor he sang special praises, lifted up prayers, and offered affections in such number and in such a manner that the human tongue cannot express it."*[316] If we examine ourselves seriously we must ask, where are these offerings to the Immaculate with *"affections in such number and in such a manner that the human tongue cannot express it?"*

THE HOLY ROSARY

Among all of the daily Marian prayers recited by those who have taken the *Marian Vow*, the Holy Rosary cannot help but be the most preferred and loved. Referring to Lourdes, St. Maximilian points out: *"The most holy Virgin* always *appeared with the Rosary."*[317] We can add with even more emphasis that in each one of the six apparitions at Fatima the Immaculate expressly recommended the prayer of the Rosary: *"Pray the Rosary."*

With regards to the Rosary, it is interesting to note that in 1818, when the body of our Seraphic Father St. Francis was exhumed, they found at his feet a crown composed of 30 beads; was this perhaps a Marian proto-Rosary? It is a legitimate question, since it is well known that St. Francis knew St. Dominic, and it is very meaningful in a special way for us as Franciscans of the Immaculate.

St. Maximilian one day said that the *Rosary* was the true "secret" of all that he succeeded in doing, often in a prodigious manner, notwithstanding his poor health, the scarcity of means available, and the difficulty arising from misunderstandings from those who all the more ought to have understood and sustained him. Fr. Pal, his companion, bears witness that when they went out together for a walk in Rome, Fr. Maximilian "had me pray the Rosary with him."[318]

---

[316] Celano, *Second Life of St. Francis* (FF 786).
[317] SK 987 B
[318] Cf. G. Lentini, *Massimiliano Kolbe*, p. 43.

Regarding St. Pio on this point, it is sufficient to recall that he perhaps will have the record in hagiographical history as the most extraordinary Saint of the Rosary. The number of Rosaries he recited was so phenomenal as to reach even a quota of about 100 Rosaries a day by which he obtained torrents of grace for his spiritual children—that "worldwide clientele," as Pope Paul VI called it.

Moreover, in addition to the Rosary and the Crown of the seven joys and seven sorrows of our Blessed Lady, may the *Crown of the seven glories* also be found in the hands of each member of our religious family. We should make this Crown known and lead as many of the faithful as possible to pray it for the glory of the Immaculate, our divine Mother and the Queen of all.

CONCLUSION

At the end of this prolonged reflection upon the *Marian Vow* of unlimited consecration to the Immaculate, we cannot help but finish with a hymn of thanksgiving and praise to our divine Mother and Queen.

With the gift of the *Marian Vow*, as a matter of fact, we can and must say that the Immaculate has brought us to be consecrated to Her in so radical a manner as to be capable of becoming Her *"absolute property."* Simultaneously, She has united us to Herself in a love so fruitful as to *transubstantiate* us completely into Her, into Her very being and acting.

In this way, the *Marian Vow* becomes the vow of supreme reciprocal love between the Immaculate and the consecrated soul. There is a totality of reciprocal belonging to one another: *"We,"* writes St. Maximilian, *"truly belong to Her"*[319] and are *"unlimitedly Hers, perfectly Hers"*;[320] and She, for Her part, gives Herself to us in such a measure that we come to be transfigured into Her and become, *"in a certain sense, Her very self."*[321]

The divine fruit of this mutual proprietorship is a masterpiece of grace accomplished by the Immaculate in us, bringing us to that supreme christification through the working of Her Spouse, the Holy Spirit; and this is not just any old christification, but Her christification: the *christification of the Immaculate!* St. Maximilian was right in ardently praying: *"May the knowledge of belonging completely to the Immaculate fill us with boundless joy."*[322]

May the Immaculate be glorified for this! May She be praised and blessed forever! May She be magnified and thanked eternally!

---

[319] SK 461
[320] SK 508
[321] Ibid.
[322] SK 834

The fruitful *Franciscan* "root" and stable *Franciscan* "basis" for the *Marian Vow* is present in a significant and illuminating way in recalling that beautiful page in the Franciscan Sources where Br. Leo describes the splendid vision of the *white ladder of the Immaculate*.[323] St. Maximilian recalled this many times in his writings[324] in order to comfort and sustain the friars who were turning to Mary and entrusting themselves to the divine Mother in order to climb towards the Kingdom of Heaven in the easiest, fastest, and surest way possible.

We can truly compare the *Marian Vow* in a mystical way to that *white ladder of the Immaculate* described in the Franciscan Sources. This is our desire, and the preciousness of that *white ladder of the Immaculate* is explained by our Seraphic Father, St. Francis himself. He exhorted his friars to climb the *white ladder of the Immaculate* in order to be lifted up and made holy in the easiest, most beautiful, most exalted, and sublime way possible.

We can see that the *Marian Vow* is Franciscan in nature both by its roots and its fruits: the religious family of the *Franciscans of the Immaculate* (friars and sisters) who are a new branch of the seraphic First Order. The *white ladder of the Immaculate*, which is the *Marian Vow*, has been entrusted to us and has been recognized as a constitutive *religious vow* of our Franciscan religious profession; it has been placed as the first vow, before that of obedience, poverty, and chastity, in professing the *Seraphic Rule* (and for the *Poor Clares of the Immaculate* in professing the *Rule of St. Clare;* and for the *Franciscan Tertiaries of the Immaculate* the *profession* of the evangelical life).

❦

The fundamental theological content of the *Marian Vow* presents the ineffable mystery of the Immaculate Conception, received particularly within the dimension of Mary's divine and spiritual motherhood and Her universal mediation of graces. The mystery of the Immaculate, the divine Mother and universal Mediatrix, gives the *Marian Vow* its form and decisively directs it towards the very

---

[323] *The Little Flowers of St. Francis*, Supplementary Chapter, Ch. VII.
[324] Cf. SK 461, 643, 647, 654, 821

specific and clear affirmation of the truth of Faith of Her universal mediation of all graces.

According to St. Maximilian, it is clear that the truth of Mary's universal mediation includes both the *coredemptive* aspect of acquiring redemptive grace and the *distributive* aspect of dispensing all graces.

The *coredemptive* mediation expresses Mary's personal and direct work in cooperating as the Coredemptrix united to the Redeemer "in a close and indissoluble union" (LG 53) in reacquiring divine grace which humanity lost through the "fall" of our first parents in the earthly Paradise. In fact, Mary Most Holy is our divine Mother *"in the order of grace"* (LG 61) through the *Coredemption.*

The *distributive* mediation, on the other hand, expresses Mary Most Holy's saving mission of actively dispensing all graces in union with the Mediator until the end of time for the salvation and sanctification of mankind.

The truth of Mary's universal mediation is, as a matter of fact, the most relevant and active truth in bringing to completion God's saving designs for humanity. If the other truths of the mystery of Mary, already dogmatically defined, regard more directly Mary's *person* as *Mother of God, Perpetual Virgin, Immaculate,* and *Assumed into Heaven,* then the truth of Her universal mediation regards more directly Mary's *mission* as *universal Coredemptrix* and *Dispensatrix of all graces* for the salvation of all those in need of Redemption.

All of this highlights the special value of the *Marian Vow* which especially serves to increase Christian faith in the truth of Mary's universal mediation. Those who have taken the *Marian Vow* hope, as soon as possible, to be able to see the day of its dogmatic definition, a hope which was very dear to St. Maximilian and which must be also very dear to us.

Consequently, those who have the grace of taking the *Marian Vow* should know that they are called to the highest love: the very love of the Immaculate. This love is to be given to God the Father, Son, and Holy Spirit; it is to be given to their brothers and sisters and to all creatures, especially those in most need of salvation and sanctification.

To have the very love of the Immaculate: this is precisely the work of grace of the *Marian Vow*. Through *transubstantiation* accomplished by the divine action of the Holy Spirit, the *Marian Vow* makes the soul mystically personify the Immaculate in Her being and acting. Thus, St. Maximilian sharply admonishes us to reach the point that *"not only nothing may remain in us that is not of Her, but that we may become annihilated, as it were, in Her, changed in Her, transubstantiated in Her, that She Herself may remain."*[325]

Through *transubstantiation* into the Immaculate, it must be said, the summit of all perfection is reached whereby, according to the loving designs of God, we are *"predestined to become conformed to the image of His Son"* (Rm 8:29); in other words, *christification*: we have been predestined to be *conformed to Christ*. It is precisely through this transubstantiation into the Immaculate realized through fully living out the *Marian Vow* that we can arrive at the very christification of the Immaculate; and Hers cannot be other than the *supreme christification* for the greatest glory of God and the most extensive salvation of souls.

From this we may conclude that the *marianization* brought about in those faithfully living the *Marian Vow* is the matrix of their *christification*, just as Mary's motherhood is the pure matrix of Christ Her Son. *Marian Vow—marianization—christification,* therefore, are the three innate realities of the vocation, mission, spirituality, and seraphic holiness of the Franciscans of the Immaculate (Friars, Sisters, Poor Clares, and Tertiaries of the Immaculate).

In the end, the most profound and vital fruit of the *Marian Vow* is the life of loving union with the Immaculate. This union is entirely animated by the special, real, and mysterious "presence" of the Blessed Virgin in the life and soul of those consecrated to Her by means of the *Marian Vow*.

It can and must be said that by this special "presence" which characterizes the loving bond between the Immaculate and the soul

---

[325] SK 508

consecrated by means of the *Marian Vow*, the life of union with Her acquires a concrete, natural character of love spontaneously flowing from the deep recesses of those "possessed" by the Immaculate as Her *"absolute property."*

Therefore, that which is absolutely necessary and most important for the full fruitfulness of the *Marian Vow* is faithful correspondence. The soul must correspond without reserve to the invasion of grace which leads to *transubstantiation* into the Immaculate. Thus, she reaches the most perfect and sublime *christification*, which is the very christification of the Immaculate Herself.

The models and masters of this *christification* through the Immaculate are our heavenly Patrons: our Seraphic Father St. Francis of Assisi, our Holy Mother St. Clare of Assisi, St. Maximilian M. Kolbe, and St. Pio of Pietrelcina. These four Saints form the splendid quadrille of the *Marian Vow*. All to the praise and glory of the Immaculate Mediatrix. AMEN.

WORKS CITED

Dante Alighieri, *Paradiso*

Ven. Fr. Gabriel M. Allegra
- *Il Cuore Immacolato via a Dio* [English version: *Mary's Immaculate Heart: a way to God*, Chicago 1985]
- *Vita*

G. Cittadini, *Santa Veronica Giuliani nella luce dei Processi*, 1997

St. Bonaventure
- *De Nativitate B.M.V.*, sermo III (*Opera Omnia*, vol. IX)
- *De Purificatione B.M.V.*, sermo I (*Opera Omnia* vol. IX)
- *In III Sententiarum*, d.6, art.2, q.1, ad 2 (*Opera Omnia* vol. III)
- *De triplici via* (*Opera Omnia* vol. VIII) [English title: *The Threefold Way*, in St. Bonaventure, *Writings on the Spiritual Life*, St. Bonaventure NY 2006, pp. 81–135]
- *Leggenda maggiore*, in *Fonti Francescane*, Padua, Italy 1988 [Latin original: *Legenda Maior*, in *Opera Omnia*, vol. VIII; English title: *Life of St. Francis of Assisi*, or *Legenda maior*]

St. Clare of Assisi
- *Regula*, in *Fonti Francescane*, Padua, Italy 1988 [English title: *Rule*]
- *Lettere*, in *Fonti Francescane*, Padua, Italy 1988 [English title: *Letters*]
- *Processo di Canonizzazione*, in *Fonti Francescane*, Padua, Italy 1988 [English title: *Process of Canonization*]
- *Bolla di Canonizzazione*, in *Fonti Francescane*, Padua, Italy 1988 [English title: *Bull of Canonization*]

V. Di Lillo, *Incontri con Padre Massimiliano*, Pescara, Italy 1984 [English: *Roman Conferences of St. Maximilian M. Kolbe*, New Bedford MA 2004]

St. Ephrem, *Oratio*

St. Francis of Assisi

- *Regule* ed *esortazioni*, in *Fonti Francescane*, Padua, Italy 1988 [English titles: *Rules* and *Admonitions*]
- *Laudi* e *preghiere*, in *Fonti Francescane*, Padua, Italy 1988 [English titles: *Praises* and *Prayers*]

Servant of God Pope John Paul II, *Redemptoris Mater*

G. Lentini, *Massimiliano Kolbe il campione dell'Immacolata*, Rome 1989

St. Louis M. de Montfort:
- *Il segreto di Maria* [English: *The Secret of Mary*]
- *Trattato della vera devozione alla santa Vergine* [*True Devotion to the Blessed Virgin*]

Servant of God Sr. Lucia, *Gli appelli del messaggio di Fatima*, Coimbra, Portugal 2002 [English: *'Calls' from the Messages of Fatima*]

St. Maximilian M. Kolbe:
- *Gli scritti di san Massimiliano Kolbe,* Rome, Italy 1997 [abbrev. SK; no complete translation exists in English]
- *Konferencje ascetyczne*, Niepokalanow 1976 [abbrev. CK; no complete translation exists in any language]

Fr. Emil Neubert, *La vita di unione con Maria,* Catania, Italy 1956 [English: *Life of Union with Mary*, Milwaukee 1959]

Ven. Fr. J.-J. Olier, *Autobiografia* [The French original can be found in the *Opera Omnia* published by Migne in Paris during the 19th century]

St. Pio of Pietrelcina
- *Epistolario*, vol. I and IV, San Giovanni Rotondo, Italy 2002 [Available in English (in three separate volumes): *Letters: correspondence with his spiritual directors (1910–1922)*, Foggia 1985; *Letters by Padre Pio*, Foggia 1985; *More Letters by Padre Pio*, Foggia 1985]
- *Padre Pio parla della Madonna*, S. Giovanni Rotondo, Italy 2006

Fr. Severino Ragazzini, *Maria vita dell'anima*, Frigento, Italy 1982

Fr. Johannes Schneider, *Virgo Ecclesia Facta. The Presence of Mary in the Crucifix of San Damiano and in the* Office of the Passion *of St. Francis of Assisi*, New Bedford 2004.

Bl. Thomas of Celano
- *Leggenda di santa Chiara*, in *Fonti Francescane*, Padua, Italy 1988 [English title: *Legend of St. Clare*]
- *Vita prima di san Francesco d'Assisi*, in *Fonti Francescane*, Padua, Italy 1988 [English title: *First Life of St. Francis of Assisi*]
- *Vita seconda di san Francesco d'Assisi*, in *Fonti Francescane*, Padua, Italy 1988 [English title: *Second Life of St. Francis of Assisi*]

P. Treece, *A Man for Others. Maximilian Kolbe, the "Saint of Auschwitz" in the Words of Those Who Knew Him*, New York 1982.

Vatican II, *Lumen Gentium*

St. Veronica Giuliani, *Diario*, vol. VI and IX, Prato, Italy 1905–1927

Fonti Francescane, Padua, Italy 1988. Abbreviated FF.

- *Leggenda dei tre compagni* [English title: *The Legend of the Three Companions*]
- *I fioretti* [English title: *The Little Flowers of St. Francis*]
- *Sacrum Commercium sancti Francisci cum Domina Paupertate* [English title: *The Sacred Commerce of St. Francis with Lady Poverty*]
- Cf. other citations listed above by St. Bonaventure, St. Clare, St. Francis, and Bl. Thomas of Celano: English versions of all these can be found in the English equivalents of the *Fonti Francescane*: cf. below under the titles of *Omnibus*, or *Early Documents* [for St. Francis, 3 vols., and St. Clare, 1 vol.]

English equivalents of the ***Fonti Francescane***:

1) *English Omnibus of the Sources for the Life of St. Francis*, Chicago 1973;

2) *St. Francis of Assisi. Early Documents.* Vol. I: *Saint*; Vol. II: *Founder*; Vol. III: *Prophet*, New York 1999–2001;

3) *St. Clare of Assisi. Early Documents*, New York 2006